Chas. W. Fitts

The Universal Cook Book

Compiled from the Tested Recipes of Practical Cooks

Chas. W. Fitts

The Universal Cook Book
Compiled from the Tested Recipes of Practical Cooks

ISBN/EAN: 9783744788700

Printed in Europe, USA, Canada, Australia, Japan

Cover: Foto ©Lupo / pixelio.de

More available books at **www.hansebooks.com**

"We Grow Like What we Eat. Bad Food Depresses, and Good Food Exalts us Like an Inspiration."

THE

UNIVERSAL COOK=BOOK,

COMPILED FROM

THE TESTED RECIPES OF

PRACTICAL COOKS.

COMPILED BY

MRS. CHAS. W. FITTS,

WASHINGTON, D. C.

AGE PRINTING COMPANY, 8th and H Sts., N. W., Washington, D. C.

A Receipt for One Dozen

PHOTOGRAPHS

TAKEN BY

J. D. BOYCE,

◎—Photographer,—◎

1113 F St.   Northwest.

Is guaranteed to give satisfaction.

Life-size Portraits of all kinds.

Interior and Exterior Views.

Railroad Scenery, Bridges, Machinery, &c.

Old Pictures Copied Any Size,

Neatness.
Promptness.
Attention.

SHOULD YOU LIKE TO BE

FITTED

With a Comfortable Shoe.

Stoll's Shoe Palace

Can Furnish Them At a Very

SMALL COST

807 7th Street, N. W.

NEXT DOOR TO KING'S PALACE

"CERES."

Best in the World.

Housekeepers, do you want the best bread obtainable? If so, use, "CERES" Flour in your bread making and you will have bread that will be the envy of your neighbors. Everybody who has used "CERES" Flour says that it makes "more" bread, "lighter" bread, "sweeter" bread, "whiter" bread and "better" bread than any other flour. Tell your grocer that you will have "CERES" Flour and that you'll accept no substitute. We will tell you a way so you can be positive that you are getting the genuine "CERES." Look for the circular signed in autograph by Wm. M. Galt & Co., and bearing the imprint of two gold medals, which is contained in every sack of "CERES" Flour. "CERES" for sale by all grocers. We only wholesale "CERES."

Wm. M. Galt & Co.,

Wholesale Flour and Feed Dealers,

Cor. 1st and Indiana Ave., N. W.

The Compiler of this book has used the CERES FLOUR and recommends its use for bread and pastry.

THE UNIVERSAL COOK-BOOK.

CONTENTS.

Introductory	viii
Soups	1
Fish and Shell Fish	13
Meats	29
Poultry and Game	51
Vegetables	67
Salads	83
Pickles and Meat Sauces	91
Cheese	101
Eggs	105
Bread	113
Pies	129
Puddings and Sauces	137
Desserts and Fancy Dishes	147
Cakes	153
Preserves and Jellies	167
Candies	171
Miscellaneous	173
Index to Advertisers	177

EACH and EVERY CAN OF

IMPERIAL
BAKING POWDER.
PERFECT  PURITY

Is guaranteed in every respect as to Quality and Purity, and dealers are authorized to refund the purchase money should parties have cause for complaint.

This Powder contains no ALUM, AMMONIA, or any INJURIOUS SUBSTANCE whatsoever, the principal component part being ABSOLUTELY PURE CREAM TARTAR, and other materials in chemical proportion.

From our knowledge of the articles used by us in the manufacture of the IMPERIAL BAKING POWDER, and from the opinion of high authorities who have tested the same, **WE CONFIDENTLY CLAIM THAT THE IMPERIAL IS UNSURPASSED BY ANY BAKING POWDER ON THE MARKET.**

This may seem to be a bold assertion, but we know it to be a FACT.

We do not intend to spend FABULOUS AMOUNTS in advertising, but propose to give the BENEFIT of this ENORMOUS EXPENSE to the CONSUMER in the price of the article.

The Cheapest end Best High Grade Baking Powder
ON THE MARKET IS THE
IMPERIAL.
ASK YOUR GROCER FOR IT.

1 lb. cans, 40 cents.   ½ lb. cans, 20 cents.   3 oz. cans, 10 cents.

INTRODUCTORY.

Ladies:

The Universal Cook Book is before you. While it does not aspire to a place among kindred books by noteworthy authors, the Compiler feels moved to say that she trusts that its carefully selected recipes of proven merit may entitle it to "honorable mention" in the kitchen.

That she is able to place this book in your hands, is due to the substantial support and encouragement which she has received from the members of the Ladies' Aid of the Church of Our Father, to whom this book is respectfully dedicated.

THE COMPILER.

December 5, 1894.

DROP THAT POSTAL

now!
asking our wagon to call Monday.
We have the facilities, the machinery the experience and the will to give you better service than any other laundry in Washington. We study YOUR INTERESTS. We soon found that Potomac water wasn't clean enough to wash your clothes. WE NOW USE ONLY FILTERED ARTESIAN WELL WATER.
The best washing ingredients that money can buy are none too good for your washing. We'll never be satisfied till you patronize us -- neither will you.

Lace Curtains Hand Laundered 50c. up.

YALE Steam Laundry,

F. H. WALKER & CO.,
Main Branch, 514 10th St.,
Plant, 43 G St. N. W.
'Phone, 1092.

SOUPS.

"Now good digestion wait on appetite, and health on both."
                                                SHAKESPEARE.

Soups can be made from fresh fish, flesh or fowl, vegetables, water or milk, and from odds and ends of all. Have always on hand whole and ground spices, sweet herbs, celery-seed, parsley, onions, carrots and turnips; rice, barley, tapioca, corn starch and flour; thicken and enrich.

In seasoning soup, for every quart of water use a teaspoonful of salt, one-eighth as much black pepper, two or three pepper-corns, a pinch of celery-seed, a teaspoonful of mixed herbs, loose teaspoonful of parsley, half a pint of mixed vegetables. Vegetables, if not cooked before, go in with the meat. First fry the vegetables in a little butter; it gives a "tasty" flavor.

In making stock, use a quart of water for every pound of meat and bone. Cut the meat in pieces, crack the bones, place all in the kettle, pour over it the proper quantity of cold water; let it soak awhile on the back of the range before cooking. Let soup boil slowly, never hard. Some tart apple is good in soup. When all is thoroughly done, strain through a sieve or coarse cloth; do not squeeze the cloth. If too thick, thin before using. Soup stock can be kept several days in cold weather. Put the vegetables in the day you use it; it keeps better without them. Never let the fat remain on your soup. Let it get cold and lift it off; or skim it off if hot.

Soup stock can be made clear by adding, when cold, the white and shell of one egg for each quart of stock. Set it on the fire and stir till hot, let simmer ten minutes, then add a cup of cold water and strain through a fine strainer or napkin. Serve with lemon shaved thin, croutons, force-meat balls, or hard yolk of egg.

In thickening soups, use corn-starch or flour rubbed with butter. Add catsup or sauces just before using.

The fine delicate flavor of many soups you have eaten was produced entirely by a delicious combination of seasonings. Bouquets of herbs for flavoring soups are made by tying a small bay leaf, a blade of mace, a sprig of any dry sweet herb (except sage) and a dozen pepper corns in the midst of a little bunch of parsley leaves and winding with twine, or enclosing it in a tarletan bag.

Asparagus Soup.

Take a knuckle of veal, cut in small pieces. Boil 2 hours with a small piece of salt pork. Take 2 or 3 bunches of asparagus cut up in small pieces, and put all but the heads in the soup; boil 1 hour longer, then strain; return to the fire and add the heads, boil until they are tender, season with pepper, serve in the tureen with toast.

Beef Soup.

Boil soup bone day before wanting it; skim grease off next day, and melt jelly; add spices to taste, little brandy, small teacupful of butter rubbed in browned flour, little vermicelli, and grated carrot. Boil 3 eggs hard, mash smooth, put in tureen, and pour soup over them.

Bouillon.

Six pounds of beef and bone. Cut up the meat and break the bones; add 2 quarts of cold water and simmer slowly 5 hours. Strain through a fine sieve, removing every particle of fat. Season only with pepper and salt.

Mothers! we want you to have a look at our stock of Boys' Clothing. We think we can "stretch out" your dollars for you.

SAKS & CO., Pa. Ave. & 7th St.

G. W. STORY
HEADQUARTERS FOR
BUTTERINE
In K St. Market

Also Dealer in CANNED GOODS and COTOSUET

Stands 549 & 551.   Open every day.

W. D. CLARK & CO.,
DEALERS IN
FIRST-CLASS DRY GOODS,
No. 811 Market Space, Penn. Avenue,
WASHINGTON, D. C.

J. RICHARD RIGGLES & BRO., 712 K Street N. W.
DEALERS IN
Paint, Oil, Window and Looking Glass.

Gold and Silver Bronze, Floor Stain, Prince's Metallic Roof Paint. Agents for Harrison Bros. Town and Country Mixed Paints, Philadelphia, Pa.

Bean Soup.

Soak a quart of beans over night, put them on the fire next morning with 2 quarts of cold water and about 1 pound of salt pork, boil three hours. Shred into it a head of celery, add pepper; simmer half an hour longer. Strain through a colander, serve hot.

Consomme.

(Mrs. Rorer.)

Four pounds beef; 1 ounce suet; 1 small onion; 3 quarts cold water; 4 cloves; 1 small carrot; a piece of celery; 1 egg white.

Cut into dice four pounds of lean beef from the round: put about one ounce of suet and one small onion, sliced, into the soup-kettle and cook until a good brown; then add the meat, cook without covering thirty minutes; add the cold water, cover the kettle and simmer gently for about three hours; at the end of this time add the cloves, carrot, a piece of celery, and simmer one hour longer. Strain and stand away to cool. When cold, remove all grease from the surface. Turn the consomme into a kettle; beat the white of egg with a half-cupful of cold water, add it to the boiling consomme, boil one minute and strain through cheese-cloth. Season, and it is ready to serve.

Corn Soup.

Is made the same as bean soup. Corn and beans may be used together and make a very nice soup.

Clam Soup.

Take 30 clams, draw off the liquor, put it in the kettle with a quart of water ½ teaspoonful of pepper. When it boils add the clams, boil ½ an hour, then add 2 pints of hot milk, 2 tablespoonfuls of butter, give one boil, serve hot.

Celery Soup.

Two quarts of white stock. Wash and trim 3 heads of white celery. Boil until tender in the stock, rub through a sieve, return to the stock, thicken with a dessert spoonful of corn starch and 1 of flour, mixed in a pint of milk. Add a lump of butter, salt to taste, and serve when hot.

Chicken Vegetable Soup.

(Mrs. Owens.)

Get a fat hen. After washing, put it whole into a porcelain kettle with a gallon of water; boil two hours; slice 3 or 4 Irish potatoes; 1 large onion; 1 or 2 tablespoonfuls of chopped parsley; 1 teaspoonful celery-seed, and a bit of summer savory, if you have it; ½ red pepper pod, salt to taste. When the soup has boiled one hour add the vegetables, and when nearly done put in a pint of sweet milk.

French Soup.

(Miss Wister.)

To a rich broth (for six persons), add 3 eggs; 2 teaspoonfuls flour; 1 teacupful milk.

Beat flour, milk and eggs together and pour slowly through a small sieve into the boiling broth, add a little chopped parsley and serve.

Green Pea Soup.

Put 2 quarts green peas with 4 quarts water, boil 2 hours, keeping steam waste supplied by fresh boiling water—strain them from liquor, return that to pot, rub the peas through sieve, chop an onion fine, and small sprig mint, let boil 10 minutes, stir a tablespoonful flour into 2 of butter, add pepper and salt to taste, stir smoothly into boiling soup. Serve with well buttered toasted bread.

Lobster Soup.

Three pints of white stock, boil up and thicken with a little blended flour; put in 2 ounces of butter, and stir in gradually the yolks of 2 eggs. Add half a tin of lobster, let stand ten minutes to keep hot, and serve.

Macaroni Soup.

Four pounds veal; 4 quarts cold water; ½ pound macaroni; ½ pint cream.

To about four pounds of a joint of veal or beef which must be well broken up, add the cold water and set to boil. Prepare the macaroni by boiling in a vessel by itself, with sufficient water to cover it. Add a small piece of butter to the macaroni, when tender. Strain the soup and season to taste with salt and pepper. Then add the macaroni with the cream and celery flavor.

Noodle Soup.

(Miss Wister.)

A chicken; 3 quarts water; 1 onion; bay leaf; chopped parsley for the soup; 2 eggs; enough flour to make a stiff dough; 1 saltspoonful salt for the noodles.

Put the chicken in the cold water, bring it to the boiling point and let it simmer for three hours, adding the onion, bay leaf and parsley when the chicken is about half done. Remove the chicken when thoroughly cooked—which may be served as boiled chicken or used for chicken salad. Add the noodles, boil fifteen minutes, add salt and pepper and serve.

To make the noodles, beat the eggs light, add the flour, enough to make a stiff dough, knead it well, roll out thin as a wafer, then roll up into a close roll and cut into slices about an eighth of an inch thick; spread on the board to dry for an hour or more. If this quantity is more than is needed for the soup, it will keep for several days.

C. W. DORMAN,
Washington Homœopathic Pharmacy.

(Successor to Boericke & Tafel.)

1007 H Street, Northwest, WASHINGTON, D. C.

C. M. SMOOT

Northwest Corner Third and E Streets Northeast.

✷ Fancy Groceries,
Choice Meats; Vegetables and Fruits.

Fish and Oysters in Season.

B. T. Trueworthy, Jr.,
DEALER IN

FANCY GROCERIES,
136-138 K ST. MARKET

HOME-MADE MINCEMEAT AND CATSUP A SPECIALTY.

OPEN EVERY WEEK-DAY.

BRIGHTWOOD DAIRY.

A. G. & D. G. Mount,
DEALERS IN

Fresh Milk and Cream.

Corner of 10th Street and Mass. Avenue, N. W.

Ox-Tail Soup.

An ox-tail, 2 pounds lean beef, 4 carrots, 3 onions, thyme and parsley, pepper and salt to taste, 4 quarts cold water. Cut tail into joints, fry brown in good dripping. Slice onions and 2 carrots and fry in the same, when you have taken out the pieces of tail. When done tie them, the thyme and parsley in lace bag, and drop into the soup pot. Put in the tail, then the beef cut into strips. Grate over them 2 whole carrots, pour over all the water and boil slowly 4 hours; strain and season; thicken with brown flour wet with cold water; boil 15 minutes longer and serve.

Potato Soup.

(Emma L. Hart.)

Six potatoes, 1 onion, 1 bunch celery cut fine. Boil in small quantity water till tender, pass through a sieve, add 2 quarts boiling milk, season with salt, butter and pepper. Add 1 egg beaten stiff, serve hot.

Pea Soup.

Split peas, one quart, two pounds salt pork; five quarts of water; boil five hours and strain through sieve hot.

Potage a la Reine.

To 1 quart stock add 1 pint sweet cream heated, not boiled, thicken with a little blended flour. Add ½ can boiled French peas just before serving.

Pot-Pourri.

(Miss Wister.)

A knuckle of veal; corn cut from six ears; 1 quart okra; ¼ peck tomatoes, skinned and cut into small pieces; 1 small head cabbage; 2 onions; 2 carrots; 2 turnips; thyme, parsley and summer savory—all chopped fine.

Add to the meat, vegetables and herbs, six quarts of water, with pepper and salt to taste, and let all cook slowly for three hours. This is a dinner in itself, and a good one.

Tomato Soup.

One quart can of tomatoes, two tablespoonfuls of flour, one of butter, one-half teaspoonful of salt, one of sugar, one pint of hot water, (or one quart of soup stock) a little red pepper. Let the tomato and stock, (or water,) come to a boil, rub flour, butter and a little of the tomato together, and stir into the boiling mixture. Strain through a sieve fine enough to retain the seeds. Butter slices of stale bread, cut in small squares, place in a tin pan buttered side up, and brown in a quick oven. Serve with the soup.

Mock Turtle Soup.

Boil a calf's liver and heart with a knuckle of veal for three or four hours, skimming well, then strain off. Chop the meat fine, and add to it a chopped onion, salt, pepper and ground cloves to taste, thickening, if necessary, with a little browned flour, cooking again in the liquor. Have the yolks of four or five hard boiled eggs cut up for the tureen; also slices of lemon.

Stock.

4 pounds of beef or a shin of beef, 1 gallon of cold water and 2 teaspoonfuls of salt. Put it on the back of the stove and slowly come to a boil, and keep boiling until the water is boiled away $\frac{1}{2}$, strain and set it to cool; when cool take the grease off the top and it is ready for use. This stock will keep 1 week in cold weather.

MEMORANDA.

MEMORANDA.

BROMO PEPSIN
is the only sure cure for Headache from any cause. 10 cents at drug stores.

Prepared by F. M. CRISWELL.

GEO. T. BUDD,
Confectioner and Caterer,
510 Ninth Street Northwest,
WASHINGTON, D. C.

BRANSON and TARBELL
(Successors to J. F. Russell,)

Staple & Fancy Groceries,
NO LIQUORS. Foreign Fruits and Imported Delicacies.

COR. NINTH AND H STS., N. W.

SAMPSON'S DAIRY, Thomas Sampson, Proprietor
No 1003 New York Avenue, N. W., Washington, D. C.
Best Quality of Milk and Cream, Butter, Eggs, and Cottage Cheese.

FISH AND SHELL FISH.

"Master, I marvel how the fishes live in the Sea?"
"Why, as men do on land; the great ones eat up the little ones."
PERICLES.

How to select Fish.

In selecting fish at the market see that the gills are red, the eyes full, the body of the fish firm, and the fins stiff.

Salt mackerel and other small salt fish should be broiled. Small pan fish and steaks of large white dry fish are good fried. Fresh salmon, mackerel, and blue fish are oily fish and should not be fried. Boil oily fish if large—broil them if small. Cod, haddock, blue fish, small salmon, bass, and shad may be stuffed and baked whole.

Serve fish with bread and potatoes, and cucumbers, if in season.

Cream and egg sauces, lobster, oyster, shrimp, tartar and piquante sauces are served with boiled fish.

Fry fish and oysters in very hot salt pork fat. Oil is better but very expensive.

Fish may be scaled much easier by dipping into boiling water about one minute.

Oysters are best roasted in the shell, convex side downward to hold the juices, and cooked till they will open well.

Baked Shad.
(Mrs. C. W. F.)

Make a dressing of bread crumbs, 2 tablespoonfuls of minced

onion, some chopped parsley, a little butter, 1 teaspoonful of chopped suet, pepper and salt, sage and a beaten egg. Wet with milk. Stuff the fish and sew or tie securely. Place in a pan with some hot water; lay pieces of salt pork on top with a little pepper and salt, and bake, basting *very often*.

Fried Blue Fish and other kinds.

Clean, wipe dry, inside and out. Sprinkle with flour, and season with salt. Fry in hot butter or sweet lard, ½ lard and ½ butter make a good mixture for frying fish. The moment fish are done to good brown, take them from fat and drain in hot strainer; garnish with parsley.

To Fry Brook Trout or Any Other Small Fish.

Clean fish, and let them lie a few minutes wrapped singly in clean dry towel; season with pepper and salt; roll in corn meal, fry in ⅓ butter and ⅔ lard; drain on sieve, and serve hot.

Broiled Halibut.

Slices of halibut, salt, pepper, butter. Cut the slices of fish about an inch thick, season with pepper and salt, and lay them in melted butter ½ hour, allowing 3 tablespoonfuls of butter to a pound of fish, then roll them in flour, and broil about 20 minutes. Serve very hot.

Boiled Fish.
(Mrs. C. W. F.)

Sew the fish in thin cloth fitted to shape, boil in salted water (boiling from the first) allow 15 minutes to the pound. Unwrap and pour over it the following sauce.

Sauce For Boiled Fish.

To 1 gill boiling water add as much milk; stir into this while boiling 2 tablespoonfuls butter gradually, 1 tablespoonful flour wet up with cold water; as it thickens, the chopped yelk of 1 boiled egg and 1 raw egg beaten light. Take directly from fire, season with pepper, salt, a little chopped parsley and juice of 1 lemon, and set covered in boiling water (but not over fire) 5 minutes, stirring occasionally. Pour part of sauce over fish when dished; the rest in a boat. Serve mashed potatoes with it.

Fish Cutlets.

Use a pint of cold broiled fish; this should be mixed with a cream sauce and the yolks of 2 eggs; when this mixture is quite cold it can readily be made into croquettes. These should be dipped into the beaten white of an egg, to which has been added just a little water; then cover them with bread crumbs; never use fine crumbs for frying: the coarse crumbs act as a sponge in absorbing the fat, and thus leave the croquettes perfectly dry, as they should be; you would be surprised to know how little fat is required for frying; it requires only a few moments to brown the cutlets in the fat.

Cream Fish.

Three pounds haddock, 1 pint of cream, ½ pound of butter, 1 tablespoonful of flour. Boil your fish with plenty of salt in the water. When cooked, skin it and take out all the bones. Flake with a fork. Heat the cream, season it, and put ½ large onion in it. Beat your butter and flour to a cream, and add the mixture, boiling fifteen minutes. Butter a large baking dish, put in a layer of fish and one of dressing, making sure to have the dressing on top. Cover with bread crumbs, putting small pieces of butter on top and brown nicely. Milk will do as well as cream if it is rich.

· Mayonaise Fish.

Take a pound or so of cold boiled fish (halibut or cod), cut into small pieces; then make the dressing as follows: the yolks of 2 boiled and 2 raw eggs rubbed to a smooth paste with salad oil; add to these, salt, pepper, a very little mustard, 2 teaspoonfuls of white sugar, and lastly 6 tablespoonfuls of vinegar; beat the mixture until light, and just before pouring it over the fish stir in lightly the frothed white of a raw egg. Serve the fish in a dish with lettuce leaves around the edges; half of the sauce mixed with the fish, the rest thrown over the top.

Cod Fish Stew.

(Mrs. Owens.)

Cut up into inch pieces, allowing ½ teacupful to a pint of milk. Put on the stove in a stew pan or spider, well covered with cold water. When it comes to a boil, drain and pour in a pint or quart of milk, according to size of family. When hot, thicken with a tablespoonful of flour made smooth with cold milk or water. An egg broken in and stirred rapidly at the last is an improvement. Season with a teaspoonful of butter. Serve with baked potatoes.

Codfish Balls.

(Mrs. H. S. B.)

A pound of *firm white* salt codfish, 6 medium-sized potatoes, ½ a teacup of milk, 1 egg, a full tablespoonful of butter. Put the fish in *cold* water and let it steep twenty minutes on the fire. Drain off the water, and pour on boiling water, letting it steep until it is sufficiently freshened. When cold, pick the fish into fine shreds with a fork, removing the skin and bones. Mash the potatoes, *which must be fresh boiled*, with the butter, add the milk and beaten egg and a little pepper, lastly the picked fish. Drop the mixture *from a spoon* into boiling lard. Never use flour in making up the balls.

Fish Chowder.

(Mrs. C. W. F.)

Five pounds of fish cut in steaks, 1 chopped onion, 4 chopped potatoes, ½ pound of salt pork, chopped. Put the pork and onions in the bottom of the kettle, let them fry brown, then

ROSE COTTAGE.

Situated on St. Patrick's Bay, three-fourths mile North of Colton's Point, Md. Open to visitors for SEASON of 1895, on MAY 1st.

A fine Orchard of choice fruits. Water is supplied by a galvanized Steel Tower and Pump. No chills nor mosquitoes. Bathing is safe and convenient. Oysters, fish and crabs are abundant.

Visitors met by a conveyance at boat. Address all the inquiries to the undersigned, 138 E St., N. E., until May 1st thereafter, Colton's Point, Md.

ADAM FISHER,
Proprietor.

EDW. S. SCHMID,
DEALER IN

Singing Birds, Fine Breed Fowl, Cages, Pet Animals, Dog and Bird Foods, Medicines, etc.

712 12th Street, N. W.,   Branch Store, 1221 Pa. Ave. N. W.

T. JARVIS,
CONFECTIONER AND CATERER.

Ice Cream and Ices.   426 9th St., N. W.

Ladies' and Gentlemen's Cafe open till 11 P. M.
Personal attention given to serving Weddings, Receptions, &c.

put a layer of fish, well seasoned with salt and pepper, then a layer of potatoes, and so on until the ingredients are used. Pour on 3 quarts of water and boil half an hour. Soak ½ dozen crackers in a pint of milk in the tureen and pour the chowder over them.

Clam chowder is made in the same way, using 25 chopped clams, no salt, and a tablespoonful of tomato catsup.

Sauce For Salmon and Other Fish.

One cupful milk heated to a boil and thickened with tablespoonful corn starch previously wet up with cold water, the liquor from the salmon, : great spoonful butter, 1 raw egg beaten light, juice ½ lemon, mace and cayenne pepper to taste. Add the egg to thickened milk when you have stirred in butter and liquor; take from fire, season and let stand in hot water 3 minutes, covered. Lastly put in lemon juice and turn out immediately. Pour it all over and around the salmon.

Oyster Short Cake.

(Mrs. Parker).

Make a good short cake and bake on pie-plates, put a quart of oysters on a stove with a little water, half a cup of milk, 2 tablespoonfuls butter, salt and pepper; thicken with a tablespoonful of flour. When the cakes are baked, split and spread the oysters between and some on top.

Fried Oysters.

Select the largest and drain them on a cloth, then dip them in rolled crackers; fry in either butter or lard until they are a nice brown, and season with pepper and salt.

Steamed Oysters.

Select large oysters, drain and place in steamer over kettle of boiling water. When done, season with pepper and salt, and serve hot on soft buttered toast.

Scalloped Oysters.

(Mrs. M. C. Currier.)

Butter an earthen pudding dish, and fill with alternate layers of crushed crackers and oysters—the first layers should be the crushed crackers—wet them with a mixture of the oyster liquid and milk. Then a layer of oysters, which sprinkle with salt, pepper, and small bits of butter the size of walnuts. Let the top layer be of crumbs, and to pour over it, and put bits of butter over it Bake about twenty minutes.

Panned Oysters.

Put a piece of butter size of an egg on a frying pan, brown and add one quart of dry oysters. When partly cooked add a tablespoonful of blended flour, salt and pepper.

Pickled Oysters.

(Mrs. H. D. Bates.)

200 oysters, 1½ pints white vinegar, 5 dozen whole cloves, 5 dozen whole peppers, 1 teaspoonful whole mace, salt to taste. Pick the oysters clean, put in a saucepan, strain their liquor over them, scald not boil them. Take out the oysters, add the vinegar and spices to the liquor and boil. When cold pour over the oysters.

Little Pigs in Blankets.

Take as many large oysters as are wished, wash and dry them thoroughly with a clean towel. Have some fat bacon cut in very thin slices, cover each oyster with them, and pin on with wooden toothpicks. Broil or roast them until the bacon is crisp and brown. Do not remove toothpicks. Serve hot.

Creamed Oysters.

To ½ tablespoonful butter, melted in a saucepan, add 1 heaping tablespoonful flour. Cook a few moments and stir in gradually 1 cup hot milk. Season with salt, pepper and 1 teaspoonful celery salt. Wash and pick over carefully one pint fine oysters, boil them in their own liquor until plump, drain, and pour over them the sauce.

Roast Oysters on Toast.

Toast some slices of bread. Wash and wipe some large fine oysters, spread as many as possible on each slice of toast, season with salt, pepper and plenty of bits of butter. Put in a hot oven until the edges of the oysters curl. Serve at once.

Oyster Pie.

(Miss Wister.)

100 oysters, drained from the liquor; 3 hard-boiled eggs; 2 ounces butter; ½ cup bread crumbs, crumbled fine; pepper, salt and powdered mace.

Line sides of a dish with pie crust, but not the bottom; then to each layer of oysters sprinkle some of the mixture. Continue this until the dish is full; then cover with crust and bake in a good oven for half an hour.

Oyster or Clam Fritters.

1½ pints of milk, 1¼ pounds of flour, 4 eggs beaten separately. Clams must be chopped small, oysters whole. Drop from spoon into hot fat.

Scallops.

Swell them in water over night; in the morning dry them in a cloth, dip in egg, then in cracker crumbs, and fry brown.

Fricasseed Lobster.

Cut the meat in small pieces, season with pepper, salt and nutmeg. Put in a stew-pan with enough water to cover it. Keep the lid close and stew.

The Microscope

A Dollar Magazine for Everybody.

In this age of progress (and of humbug) almost every article of food is at times adulterated. Any lady can learn how to detect these adulterations with the microscope. Take this magazine and begin to study the subject.

MICROSCOPICAL PUBLISHING CO.,
WASHINGTON, D. C.

DORSEY'S MARKET,

COR. 10TH AND I STS., N. W.

Choice Beef, Lamb, Veal, Pork, Poultry, Creamery Butter, Fish, Fruits, Preserves, Vegetables, and everything pertaining to a first-class market store.

FINEST QUALITY;   LOWEST PRICES.

MRS. C. W. SMILEY,

CRAYON ARTIST,

943 MASS. AVE., N. W.

SAMUEL FENTON,

———— Wholesale and Retail Dealer in ————

BEEF, * MUTTON, * LAMB

AND VEAL,

305 & 307 NORTHERN LIBERTY MARKET.

Lobster Croquettes.

Chop the meat of a boiled lobster very fine, season with pepper and salt, add bread crumbs, moisten with melted butter, make into cakes, dip them in beaten eggs, then in bread or cracker crumbs, and fry brwon in butter or lard. Croquettes may be made of cold fish, poultry or veal.

Fried Oysters.

(Mrs. M. C. Currier.)

For every egg required add two tablespoonfuls olive oil and one of water, drain and dry your oysters, roll in finely powdered bread crumbs, now dip in the egg mixture, then cracker crumbs, season with salt and pepper. Fry in as little butter as possible keeping oysters separated.

Lobster a la Newburg—No. 1.

(Mrs. M. J. Currier.)

Cut the meat of two lobsters into inch squares. Mash fine the yolks of three hard boiled eggs adding gradually two tablespoonfuls of cream or milk, put ¼ pound of butter into a sauce pan, add two tablesp onfuls of flour, mix and add ½ pint of milk or cream. Stir until ready to boil but do not boil, add yolks of eggs and lobster, stand over boiling water till lobster is heated, then add four tablespoonfuls of sherry and season with salt and pepper.

Lobster a la Newburg—No. 2.

(E. J. F.)

One large lobster, 1 tablespoon butter, 1 gill wine, 3 eggs, ½ pint cream. Cut meat lobster into small slices, put into chafing dish with butter, season well with salt and pepper, pour the wine over it; cook 10 minutes. Add the beaten yolks of eggs and the cream. Let come to a boil and serve immediately.

Creamed Salmon.

(E. J. F.)

One round-can salmon; 1 teaspoonful salt; 1 tablespoonful chopped parsley, juice half lemon, a little cayenne; one cup milk or cream, 1 tablespoonful butter, 3 tablespoonfuls of flour. Chop the salmon fine, free it from bone etc., add salt, cayenne, parsley, lemon juice and mix thoroughly, cream butter and flour together. Pour onto it the boiling milk. Stir and cook a minute until quite thick. Season slightly; mix this well with the salmon. Put into individual shells, cover lightly with bread crumbs, and bake twenty minutes. Serve immediately.

Clam Chowder.

(Mrs. J. M. Welty.)

Thirty clams, chopped; ½ dozen ordinary sized potatoes, chopped; 1 can corn; 1 can tomatoes; 1 onion, size of walnut. Teaspoonful of sage. Butter, salt and pepper to taste. Add liquor of clams and gallon of water. When above has cooked, add 1 pint sweet milk, and let whole boil. This recipe makes a *big* pot full.

Deviled Crabs.

(Mrs. Rorer).

12 nice heavy crabs; ½ pint cream; 2 tablespoonfuls flour; ¼ grated nutmeg; 4 egg yolks, boiled hard; 1 teaspoonful each of salt, butter and chopped parsley; salt and cayenne to taste.

Put the crabs in warm water; add the salt and put the kettle over a brisk fire. Boil 30 minutes. Take up and drain; break off all claws; separate the shells; remove the spongy fingers and the stomach, which is found under the head. Pick out all the meat. Put the cream on to boil, rub butter and flour together, and add to the boiling cream; stir and cook two minutes. Take from the fire, add the crab meat, the egg yolks mashed fine, parsley, nutmeg, salt and cayenne. Clear the upper shells of the crabs, fill them with the mixture, brush over with beaten egg, cover with bread crumbs and put in a quick oven to brown; or better, put them in a frying basket and plunge into boiling Cottolene until a nice brown.

Fried Smelts.

(Mrs. Rorer.)

A person who has once fried smelts in Cottolene, will never under any circumstances use lard.

Make a slight opening at the gills, then draw them between the thumb and finger, beginning at the tail. This will press out all the inside. Now dip them first in beaten eggs, then in bread crumbs and fry in very hot Cottolene. Drain, dust with salt and serve smoking hot with following sauce.

Tartar Sauce.

(Juliet Corson.)

One egg yolk; 1 level teaspoonful mustard, dry; 1 level teaspoonful salt; cayenne pepper; 1 gill salad oil; 3 tablespoonfuls lemon juice or vinegar; 1 tablespoonful each of chopped parsley, capers and gherkins; 1 teaspoonful chopped onions.

Put the yolk of a raw egg into a bowl with the mustard, salt and as much cayenne pepper as can be taken upon the point of a small penknife blade; stir these ingredients with a wooden salad spoon until they are smooth; then add a few drops at a time, the oil and lemon juice, stirring quickly all the time. When the sauce is thick and smooth, add the chopped parsley, capers and gherkins and onion; the onion must be very finely chopped. Keep cool until wanted for use.

Stewed Terrapin.

(Mrs. Rorer.)

Two terrapins; ½ pint thick cream; 6 eggs; ½ pound butter; 1

LAVENDER & ROTT,
PRODUCE DEALERS,
Stalls: 301, 302, and 303 Centre Market.

L. A. DELLWIG,
GROCER and PROVISION DEALER,
Cor. 2d and Mass. Ave. and D Sts., N. E.

Home Roasted Coffee, Home Dressed Meats, Fresh Vegetables. Full line canned goods. Goods as represented or MONEY REFUNDED.

EIKER "The Butter Man"
Can be found in all the principal Markets.
PRICES MODERATE.

J. P. V. RITTER,
DEALER IN

FLOUR AND FEED,
NO. 1321 SEVENTH STREET, N. W.

gill sherry or Madeira wine ; ¼ teaspoonful mace ; salt and cayenne to taste.

Put the terrapins alive in boiling water and boil 10 or 15 minutes, or until you can pull off the outer skin and the toe nails; put them back in fresh boiling water ; add a heaping teaspoonful of salt and boil slowly until the shells part easily and the flesh on the legs is quite tender. When done, take out, remove the under shell and let stand until cool enough to handle. Then take thick, heavy part of the intestines, and the gall sacks, which are found imbedded in one lobe of the liver, and throw them away. In removing the gall sack, be careful not to break it, as it would spoil the whole terrapin. Break the terrapin in convenient sized pieces ; cut the small intestines into tiny pieces and add to the meat ; now add the liver broken up, also all eggs found in the terrapins. Now put into a stewing-pan with the juice it has given out while being cut. Roll the butter in flour, add it to the terrapin and stand in a very moderate fire until heated. Boil the 6 eggs for 15 minutes ; take out yolks ; mash to a soomth paste with 2 tablespoonfuls of the wine, then add this, the cream and seasoning to the terrapin ; let it boil up once : take from fire, add wine and serve. It must never be boiled after adding wine. Add more or less wine to taste.

MEMORANDA.

THE RECIPES IN THIS BOOK CAN BE MOST SAT-
ISFACTORILY FILLED

BY TRADING WITH THE

Emrich Beef Company.

The Largest and most Complete Provision Markets in the District.

MAIN MARKET AND GROCERY,

1306-1312 32D Street.

BRANCH MARKETS:

3057 M Street, N. W.	5th and I Streets, N. W.
21st, and K Streets, N. W.	209 Indiana Ave., N. W.
20th St. and Pa. Ave., N. W.	1718 14th Street, N. W.
13th St. and N. Y. Ave., N. W.	14th and V Streets, N. W.
8th and M Sts., N. W.	4th and I Streets, N. W.

PHONE 347.

MEATS.

*" And now we ask what noble meat and drink,
Can help to make man work, to make him think."*

When cutting meat to cook, always cut across the grain of the muscle.

Never wash fresh meat before roasting; scrape it, if necessary to clean it. If it has been wet or moist, wipe it thoroughly dry before cooking.

Never put meat directly on the ice; put it in a vessel on ice.

If you baste roast meat, do not use salt in the basting.

Salt and season boiling meats while cooking.

In boiling, put fresh meats in hot water, and salt meats in cold water; boil both slowly.

Never salt and pepper boiling meats while cooking. Season with salt, pepper, and butter after removing from the gridiron.

An ordinary pan is good for boiling; heat very hot; use no fat of any kind; put the meat flat on the pan, turn rapidly and often, and you will find a "pan broil" very good; season when done.

A pod of red pepper in the water will prevent the unpleasant odor of boiling from filling the house. The garnishes for meats are parsley, slices of lemon, sliced carrot, sliced beets and currant jelly.

Time-table for Meats.

A quarter of lamb will roast in an hour.

A loin of veal will take two or three hours.

A loin of mutton will roast in two hours.

A leg of mutton requires from two to three hours, according to size.

A small turkey will boil in one and a quarter hours; medium in two hours; large in two and a half or three hours.

A beef tongue should be soaked for several hours, put in cold water and boiled slowly four or five hours.

A large ham should boil four hours, a small one two hours, and be put on in cold water.

Corned beef or pickled pork requires to be boiled longer than smoked meat. It should be cooked until the bones come out easily. To tender salt meats, add a little vinegar to the boiling water.

Roast beef requires 15 minutes to the pound.

How to Roast Beef.

If the housekeeper, who asks how she can have her roast beef brown on the outside and rare and juicy within, will put her beef in a very hot oven at first, keeping the temperature as high as three hundred and fifty degrees or more for half an hour, then reducing the heat to about two hundred and fifty degrees for the remainder of the time of cooking, she will attain the desired result. Of course the meat must be basted as often as every fifteen minutes. The great heat at first hardens as well as browns the surface of the piece of meat. This keeps in the juices. But if the high temperature be continued, the hardening process goes beyond the surface, and the result will be a hard, dry and stringy piece of meat. Salt when done.

Roast Beef.

Rib roast is best. Have butcher saw off about ½ bone. Cut ends of ribs clear of meat; fold flap neatly around to thick part and secure with skewers. The trimmings are yours. As meat is weighed first, take it all—will make good material for soup or gravy. Put beef in dripping pan; pour little boiling water over it. Rub a little salt into fat parts; roast 10 minutes for every pound. If meat has much fat on top cover fatty portion with paste made of flour and water. When nearly done remove this, dredge beef with flour, baste well with gravy. Sprinkle salt over top and serve. Pour fat from gravy, return to fire, thicken with browned gravy, season and boil up once. A roast should always be served with the following:

English Yorkshire Pudding.

One half pound of flour, 1 pint of milk, a pinch of salt, 1 teaspoonful of Baking Powder. Mix well together the baking powder, flour and salt, then add one-half the milk, and beat until perfectly smooth; then add remainder of the milk. Melt some butter or dripping in a flat tin, pour in the batter, place a joint of beef or mutton on it, and bake in a quick oven.

Pot Roast.

(Mrs. C. W. F).

Take any piece of fresh beef, lay in a flat-bottomed pot with 2 good-sized onions; cover with boiling water even with top of meat; cover the pot tightly, and let stew slowly until the water is evaporated; then turn the meat once or twice, watching, when it begins to brown, that it does not burn. Season with salt, pepper, etc., to taste.

Pot Roast.

Take a lean piece of beef. Cut a little fat from it and fry in an iron pot a few minutes. Season the beef, and sprinkle over a little flour; put in the pot and fry brown on all sides. Pour in hot water to half cover the beef, cover tightly and cook until tender. Add a little boiling water at intervals to prevent burning. Thicken the gravy, and pour around the meat on the platter.

Beef Stew with Dumplings.

Two pounds lean beef, cut into inch squares, sprinkled with salt, pepper, and 2 tablespoonfuls of flour. Cut fat from meat into small bits, put in stew pan and fry ten minutes. Cut 1 onion, 2 slices carrot, 2 small turnips in small dice and fry in hot fat for ten minutes. Put in the meat and fry till it browns, stirring to prevent burning, then pour over one large quart hot water, and set on stove where it will simmer gently two and one-half hours. Then add 2 sliced potatoes, boil ten minutes, then put in dumplings and boil hard ten minutes without lifting the cover.

Dumplings 1 pint flour, 2 teaspoonfuls of Baking Powder, ½ teaspoonful salt, ¼ cup sugar. Mix thoroughly, and wet with 1 small cup milk. Roll one-half inch thick, cut with biscuit cutter. Veal or mutton stew can be made the same as beef.

Stewed Beef.

Take the desired quantity of round beef, cut into three ounce pieces, and dredge with flour. Fry in the stew pan some beef drippings and a sliced onion. Put in the meat, and fry well stirring constantly ten minutes. Then add gradually enough water to cover the meat, season with salt, pepper, a teaspoonful each allspice, cloves and mace, a bay leaf, and a sliced lemon. Let it simmer gently four hours.

Beef's Tongue Boiled.

(Marion Harland.)

Wash a large, perfectly fresh tongue in three waters. Then cover well with boiling water; a little salt—plenty of it—and cook about twelve minutes to the pound. Strip off the skin; dish, when you have trimmed away the root, pour over it the following sauce: Strain a cup of the liquor in which the tongue

NATIONAL CAPITAL ICE CO.
DEALERS IN
KENNEBEC ICE.
Branch Office and Depot, 8th St. Wharf S. W.
BRANCH DEPOT: O St. Market, Cor. 7th & O Sts, N. W.

George S. Perrie, DEALER IN
HAMS, BACON, LARD, &c.
Stalls 256 and 355, Northern Liberty Market.
L Street Entrance.   Market Every Day.

CHAS. F. PLITT,
WATCHMAKER and JEWELER,
FINE SILVERWARE.
Graduate Optician.
1308 Seventh Street, Northwest, between N and O.

SPECIAL ATTENTION GIVEN TO REPAIRING OF ALL KINDS

W. S. DETWILER, FINE GRADES OF
BUTTER & CHEESE,
496-497 Centre Market,   19-O St., Market.
MARKETING   DELIVERED.

was boiled; set over the fire, and stir in 2 tablespoonfuls of butter cut up in flour, pepper to taste; the juice of a lemon, and when this has thickened, 2 small pickled cucumbers, chopped. This is a dish whose merits deserve to be better known.

Braised Beef.

(Miss Parloa.)

Take six or eight pounds of the round, and lard with ¼ of a pound of salt pork. Put 6 slices of pork in the bottom of the braising pan, and as soon as it begins to fry add 2 onions, ½ small carrot, and ½ small turnip, all cut fine. Cook these until they begin to brown; then draw them to one side of the pan and put in the beef which has been well dredged with salt, pepper and flour. Brown on all sides, and then add 1 quart of boiling water and a bouquet of sweet herbs; cover and cook slowly in the oven for four hours, basting every twenty minutes. Take up, and finish the gravy as for braised tongue, or, add to the gravy ½ can tomatoes and cook for ten minutes. Strain, pour around the beef and serve.

To Lard.

(Miss Parloa.)

Larding is a simple operation. The pork should be firm and young (salt of course). Cut thin, even slices parallel with the rind, and cut these in long, narrow strips that will fit into the needle. For beef, veal, turkey or chicken the strips should be about as large round as a lead pencil, and about three and one half inches long; and for birds, chops and sweet breads they should be about as large round as a match. Three slices are all that can be cut from one piece of pork, because when you go more than an inch away from the rind the pork is so tender that it will break when in the needle. Put the strips in a bowl broken ice to harden. Have the meat free from skin and gristle if beef or veal. Put a strip, also called a lardoon, into the needle as far as it will go. Push the needle through the meat, leaving about three-quarters of an inch of the strip exposed at both sides. Continue until there are a number of rows on the top of the meat.

Spiced Beef.

(Auntie Gregory.)

Chop tough beefsteak (raw) and piece of suet size of an egg. Season with pepper, salt, and a little summer savory. Add 2 eggs, ½ pt. bread crumbs, 4 or 5 tablespoons cream and a small piece of butter. Mix and work in roll, with enough flour to keep together, and bake in a pan (with a little butter and water) like a roast. Slice when cold.

Potted Beef.

The beef well boiled, all the fat taken off, chop very fine, season with salt, pepper, allspice and a little sage. Melt butter enough to knead it well together. Pack it closely in bowls and pour melted butter over it. It will keep a week in cool weather.

Broiled Beef Steak.

Cut the steak about an inch in thickness if you like it *rare*, and broil it over a quick fire until it is browned on both sides. It should be turned often while broiling to prevent burning and to save the juice. Use a wire grating. Grooved gridirons recommended to *save the gravy*, should never be used; for the *gravy* or juice of the meat should not be allowed to escape the meat until after it is dished. Season with salt and pepper after it is done, and lay your butter cold on the steak, set it in the oven a minute or two until it is melted.

Beef Steak and Potatoes.

(Mrs. Fuller.)

Take a large and tender steak, bone it, and scatter over it bits of butter, salt and pepper and a little sage and finely chopped onions. Over that spread a thick cushion of mashed potatoes, well seasoned with salt, fresh butter and a very little milk. Roll up the steak with the potatoes inside, and fasten the sides and the ends with skewers. Put the steak into a baking pan with a large cupful of stock of gravy and let it cook slowly, basting like a chicken. Serve with a rim of mashed potatoes around the platter and garnish with watercress.

Beef Steak, with Onions.

(Mrs. Parker.)

Pound the steak, season and fry; then dredge flour over it and add a cup of boiling water. Drain the onions, which must have been boiled, cut them up and put them into the pan, having taken out the steak; add a lump of butter and a little more flour, stir, and when the onions are brown, put in the steak; when thorougly heated, serve.

Beef Steak Pie (French Style).

Take a nice piece of beef, rump or sirloin; cut in small slices; slice also a little raw ham; put both in a frying-pan, with some butter and small quantity chopped onions; let them simmer together a short time on the fire or in the oven; add a little flour and enough stock to make sauce; salt, pepper, chopped parsley and a little Worcestershire sauce as seasoning; add also a few sliced potatoes, and cook together for about 20 minutes; put this into a pie-dish, with a few slices of hard boiled eggs on the top and cover with a layer of common paste. Bake from 15 to 20 minutes in a well heated oven. All dark meat pies can be treated precisely the same way. If poultry, leave the potatoes out.

Frizzled Beef.

(Miss Wister.)

One quarter of a pound dressed beef cut as thin as Saratoga potatoes; 3 ounces butter and Cottolene mixed; 2 teacupful milk; 1 tablespoonful flour.

Place butter in skillet over moderately hot fire; when it com

ECKINGTON DAIRY.
KEATING AVE.
P. A. CUDMORE,
DEALER IN
Unadulterated Milk, Cream and Buttermilk.
Fresh Country Butter and Eggs. BRANCH OFFICE, 101 B St., S. E.

IF YOU WANT
PURE UNADULTERATED BUTTER
BUY **Excelsior Creamery,**

Call or address **E. T. Gibbons,**
Sole Agent for Washington. 254 K Street Market.
DELIVERED ANYWHERE.

H. BURKHART & SON,
FURNITURE, CARPETS
Mattresses, Oil-Cloths, Mattings, Rugs, Window Shades,
Childrens' Carriages, Refrigerators, Etc.

☞ **QUICK SALES AND SMALL PROFITS.**
1013 and 1015 Seventh Street, Northwest.

C. H. BURGESS & SON,
DEALERS IN
COAL, WOOD AND COKE,
WASHINGTON, D. C.

MAIN OFFICE,	DEPOT AND STORE YARD,
Eighth and O Streets, N. W.	First and N Streets, N. E.
Telephone 450.	Telephone 550.

mences to brown add beef and sift the flour in gradually; let all cook till the flour looks brown, but be careful not to scorch; then add milk, stirring all the time, till the dressing has cooked to consistency of rich cream. This is a delicious breakfast relish, and the mixture is admirable to be eaten with griddle cakes.

Washington Steak.

(Mrs. C. W. F.)

Take a porterhouse steak, cut two inches thick and well trimmed of bone and fat, and put it on the broiler and broil quickly over a hot fire. Place it on a hot platter and spread both sides of it with this mixture: a tablespoonful of melted butter, ½ tablespoonful of salt, and ¼ tablespoonful of white pepper. On top of the steak, place 3 plantains, just fried in butter. The plantains are the red bananas. Over this pour ½ pint of bechamel sauce and over the whole sprinkle a tablespoonful of grated horse radish.

White House Steak.

(Mrs. Sprague.)

One pound of steak chopped very fine and freed from sinews and gristle. Mince fine a tablespoonful of onion and fry it a light brown in a little butter. Add the minced meat and an equal quantity of bread crumbs, season nicely, and moisten with a little cold gravy or stock of any kind. It must be just moist enough to mould into shape. Pressed in a small wine-glass they resemble pears, and after they are fried they should have a sprig of parsley inserted into the stem end; or you may roll them round like sausages or make into little flat cakes. They must be dipped in crumbs, then in beaten egg, and again in crumbs. Make a little brown gravy to pour round them, or serve with a mushroom or tomato sauce.

Boiled Mutton with Caper Sauce.

(Mrs A. G Rogers.)

Have ready a pot of boiling water, add a little salt; wash a leg of mutton and rub salt through it. Cook about three hours—according to size. Take some of the broth, thicken with flour and butter, salt, pepper and 2 tablespoonfuls of capers, or mint sauce if preferred.

Mint Sauce.

Two tablespoonfuls green mint, chopped fine, 1 tablespoonful white sugar, 1 cup best cider vinegar. Put vinegar and sugar in sauce boat and stir in mint; stand 15 minutes before serving.

Baked Leg of Mutton.

(Mrs. Parker.)

Take a leg of mutton weighing 6 or 8 pounds, cut down the under side and remove the bone, fill it with a dressing made of 4 ounces of suet, 2 of chopped ham, 6 ounces of stale bread, 2 eggs, 1 onion, a little thyme, sweet marjoram, parsley, nutmeg, salt, and pepper; sew up, lay in a pan and put in a hot oven; baste with butter, cook three hours.

Mutton Haggis.

(Mrs. Rorer.)

Chop the uncooked heart, tongue, and ½ the liver of a sheep, and mix with them ½ that weight in chopped bacon; add a ½ cup of stale bread crumbs, the grated rind of 1 lemon, 1 teaspoonful of salt, ¼ teaspoonful of black pepper, and 2 well beaten eggs; pack this into a well buttered mold, cover, place in a kettle partly filled with boiling water, and boil slowly for two hours. When done, turn it on a dish, and serve it plain or with sauce bechamel.

Roast Lamb.

Lay in dripping-pan, dash cup cold water over it, and roast in oven; time, say 10 minutes to pound. Baste often and freely, and after ½ hour cover with sheet buttered paper, 5 minutes before taking up, remove this, dredge with flour; as it browns bring to a froth with butter. Do not send gravy to table if you use mint sauce.

To Give a Delicious Flavor to Lamb.

If it is to be eaten cold, put in the water in which it is boiled whole cloves and long sticks of cinnamon. To 1 leg of lamb allow 1 small handful of cloves, and 2 or 3 sticks of cinnamon. If the lamb is to be roasted, boil the cloves and cinnamon in water, and baste the lamb with it.

Breaded Mutton Chops.

Trim neatly, cut off all fat and skin, roll in beaten egg, then in cracker crumbs, and fry in hot dripping. Turn as the under side browns, drain and serve.

Roast Fillet of Veal.

Veal, ½ pint melted butter, ½ pound force-meat, 1 lemon. Bone the joint; make deep incision between fillet and saddle, and fill with force-meat. Bind joint in round form; fasten with skewers and twine; cover with buttered paper. Roast slowly at first. Baste well; take off paper just before done, dredge over a little flour, and baste with butter. Replace skewers with silver one. Pour over melted butter with juice of lemon and brown gravy. Garnish with sliced lemon. Time, 4 hours for 12 pounds.

Veal Pot Pie.

(Mrs. Owens.)

Take 2 pounds veal—a rib piece is good—cut it in small pieces, put it into a pot, having placed a small plate in the bottom to keep the meat from burning. Put in 2 quarts of water, either hot or cold. Keep it boiling for about an hour and a half. Then make a quart of flour into biscuit dough, and a half hour before serving drop in small lumps of the dough. Be sure that there is water sufficient to cover the meat entirely, when the dumplings are put in, and cover closely for at least twenty minutes. Pota-

Every defect of vision accurately and scientifically corrected, headaches and pain in the eyes relieved. Satisfaction guaranteed in every case.

BUCHANAN BROS.
Specialists,

Washington, D. C.   1115 F St. N. W.

PHILADELPHIA STORE.

CARHART & LEIDY,

Dry Goods, ✸ Trimmings, ✸ Underware,
UPHOLSTERY, MATTINGS, OIL CLOTH, &c.

928 Seventh Street and 706 K Street Northwest.

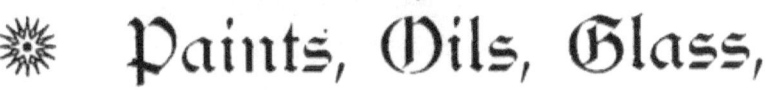

ARTIST'S MATERIALS.
S. W. COR. 7TH & N STS., N. W.

toes may be cooked with it, but we prefer them cooked separately and mashed.

Veal Loaf.

Three and one half pounds of minced veal (the leg is best for this purpose), three eggs well beaten, 1 tablespoonful of pepper and 1 of salt, 1 grated nutmeg, 4 rolled crackers, 1 tablespoonful of cream, butter the size of an egg. Mix these together and make into a loaf, roast and baste like other meats. Beef may be used in place of veal by adding ¼ pound of salt pork, minced fine.

Breaded Veal Cutlets.

("Marion Harland.")

Trim and flatten the cutlets; pepper and salt, and roll in beaten egg, then in pounded cracker. Fry rather slowly in good dripping; turning when the lower side is brown. Drain off the fat; squeeze a little lemon juice upon each, and serve in a hot, flat dish.

Calf's Liver Braised.

(Mrs. Lincoln.)

Wipe with a clean wet cloth. Lard the rounded side with bacon or salt pork. Fry 1 onion in salt pork fat. Put the liver and fried onion in a braising pan; add hot water or stock to half cover, 1 teaspoonful of salt, 1 salt-spoonful of pepper, and 1 tablespoonful of herbs. Cover, and cook in a moderate oven 2 hours, basting often. When ready to serve, strain the liquor, season with lemon juice, and pour it over the liver.

Roast Calf's Liver.

Wash thoroughly and wipe dry, cut a long deep hole in the side, stuff with crumbs, bacon and onion, chopped fine, salt, pepper and bits of butter, and one well beaten egg. Sew or tie together, lard it over and bake, serve with gravy and currant jelly.

Stewed Kidney.

Put on a kidney early in the afternoon and let simmer till bed time, allow it to remain all night in the same water. Next morning cut into small pieces, and stew for an hour or more : make a brown gravy and just before serving add 2 hard boiled eggs, sliced.

Veal Croquettes.

If for breakfast they can be prepared the night before, and so be ready for the table in a few minutes. Chop the veal fine; mix ½ cup of sweet milk with about a teaspoonful of flour. Melt a piece of butter the size of an egg, and stir the flour and milk in it; then let it come to a boil. Mix this thoroughly with the meat; form it in balls or flat cakes.

To Stew Pork.

(Miss Wister.)

Take a nice piece of the leg of fresh pork ; rub it with a little salt and score the skin. Put it into a pot with sufficient water to cover it, and stew it gently for two hours or more, according to its size. Then put into the same pot a dozen or more sweet potatoes, scraped and split and cut in pieces. Let the whole stew gently together for an hour and a half, or till it is thoroughly done. This stew will be found very good. For sweet potatoes you can substitute white ones mixed with sliced turnips, or parsnips scraped and split.

Souse of Pigs Feet.

(Mrs. Owens.)

Put the pigs' feet and ears, when well cleaned, over the fire in cold water. Boil till tender; pour over them in a jar a pickle made of cider vinegar, whole peppers, cloves and mace, boiling hot. They will be ready to eat in three days, or less.

Roast Pork.

Pork is roasted the same as beef.

Pork Chops, with Tomato Gravy.

Trim off skin and fat; rub the chops over with a mixture of powdered sage and onion; put small piece butter into a frying-pan; put in the chops and cook slowly, as they should be well done. Lay chops on hot dish; add a little hot water to gravy in pan; 1 large spoonful butter, rolled in flour; pepper, salt and sugar, and ½ cup juice drained from canned tomatoes. The tomatoes themselves can be used for a tomato omelette. Stew 5 minutes and pour over the chops and serve.

How to Boil a Ham.

Put a ham weighing ten pounds in a pot large enough to contain water enough to cover it. Bring to a boil gradually, then add 2 heads celery, 2 turnips, 3 onions, a bunch of savory herbs —the vegetables cut into dice. Let it simmer gently four hours. Remove the skin, sprinkle with pepper, put in a few cloves, and brown in a quick oven.

Boiled Ham.

Boil it 3 or 4 hours, according to size, then skin the whole and fit it for the table; then set in oven for ½ an hour, cover thickly with pounded rusk or bread crumbs, set back for ½ an hour longer. Boiled ham is always improved by setting in an oven for nearly an hour, till much of the fat dries out, and it also makes it more tender.

Ham Patties.

One pint of ham, which has been previously cooked, mix with 2 parts of bread crumbs, wet with milk. Put the batter in gem pans, break 1 egg over each, sprinkle the top thickly with cracker crumbs, and bake until browned over. A nice breakfast dish.

Meat Balls.

One bowl full of fine chopped cold meat; add 1 cup of bread or cracker crumbs, a little chopped onion, a little gravy mixed with

COOK YOUR FOOD
WITH
COAL

Bought of **G. W. Merrill & Co.,**

Office 454 N. Y. Ave.,

DEPOT AND SAW MILL 4TH AND R STS. N. E., ECKINGTON.

Hickory and other Fireplace Wood a Specialty.

GEORGE S. DONN,
Practical Paper Hanger.
PAPER HANGINGS, WINDOW SHADES, PICTURE RODS,

No. 1240 Seventh Street, Northwest,

Telephone Call, 1514.

SPECIAL!

We have just received New Raisins, Figs, Currants, Citron, New York Buckwheat, "Clover Leaf," "Salmon," New Lobster and Shrimps. We also have "Hasty Lunch," Chocolate "an excellent drink prepared in one minute."

J. H. HUNGERFORD,

Cor. 9th and O Sts.

USE GOLDEN ROD FLOUR.

the crumbs to moisten them. Season with pepper, salt, thyme or savory, and fry in balls.

New England Boiled Dinner.

(Juliet Corson.)

Remove the bone from a compact cut of the round of corned beef weighing about 8 pounds, and tie the meat as closely as possible; put it in a deep pot, cover it with cold water, add a teaspoonful of salt and half a salt spoonful of pepper ; let it boil quickly, removing all scum; when no more scum rises, put with it the following vegetables, peeled and cut in slices two inches thick ; 2 carrots, four beets, four white turnips, and 1 yellow turnip, 6 small onions peeled so that they will remain unbroken, and a large head of celery cut in two inch lengths. Place the pot where its contents will simmer slowly for two hours. A glass of wine, or any table sauce preferred, may be added before the dish is finished. To serve it, put the meat in the middle of a platter, arrange the vegetables around it, and pour a little of the gravy over it. More of the gravy should be served in a small boat, with a dish of boiled potatoes. The united flavor of the meat and vegetables characterizes the dish. Cabbage and squash can be added when preferred.

Scrapple.

(Miss Wister.)

Take such parts of the pork as are not used in packing--heart, tongue, portions of the head, etc., using about equal parts of lean and fat. Thoroughly clean them, and boil quite tender in water enough to cover the meat. When done take it up, remove the bones and thicken the water in which it was boiled with cornmeal until it is the consistency of mush. Let it boil a few minutes and season with salt, pepper and summer savory. Chop the meat and return it to the mush, add salt and pepper to the taste, and let it cook a few minutes more. Dish it out and keep in a dry, cool place. Cut in slices and fry brown in Cottolene, as needed. Buckwheat meal is sometimes used with the cornmeal.

To Prepare Tripe.

Order it the day before you wish to serve it, scrape it thoroughly, wash it in several waters, then boil in salt and water until it is perfectly tender; let it drain in a platter all night. Next day cut it in small pieces and fry in hot lard after having rolled the pieces in flour. To serve with this make a rich, brown gravy, using a little of the lard in which the tripe was fried. If for breakfast, send baked potatoes, fried apples, and tomatoes with it; the tomatoes may be canned ones, cooked; and with thin slices of toasted bread put in the bottom of the dish.

Croquettes of Sweetbreads.

Blanch and braize 1 dozen sweetbreads. When cooked, cut them in small square pieces, also ½ can of mushrooms. Put in saucepan to cook, 2 finely chopped shalots or garlic with piece of butter; add some Allemande sauce, reduce it, then add sweetbreads and mushrooms. Season with salt, pepper, nutmeg and a little chopped parsley, add the yelks of 2 eggs, stir well, then put in pan to cool. Shape them in any desired form; bread them with bread crumbs, fry in hot lard. Serve with mushroom or cream sauce. You may add beef tongues or truffles, cut in small squares.

MEMORANDA.

MEMORANDA.

FAMILY ORDERS A SPECIALTY.

D. WILLIAM OYSTER

DEALER IN

FANCY TABLE BUTTER.

340, 341 & 342 Centre Market.

SPECIALTIES.
Sheaf of Wheat Print.
Elgin Creamery.
Full Cream Cheese.
Extra Fresh Eggs.

Telephone 1285

Washington, D. C.

POULTRY AND GAME.

" It is the bounty of nature that we live; but of philosophy that we live well." SENECA.

In roasting or boiling whole any fowl, truss it—which means to draw the thighs close to the body, cross the legs at the tail and tie firmly to the body with twine, which is removed before serving; or pass the legs through a slit in the skin near the tail, and skewer the wings close to the body.

To broil, split the body down the back and lay it open.

In cutting up fowl for fricassee do not *break* the bones, *cut the joints*.

Fowls with white meat should be well cooked; fowls with dark meat may be underdone.

Flesh of game is apt to be tough when first killed. It is more tender if kept some time, or if frozen.

Clean giblets thoroughly; cook and chop them fine; use them in the gravy or in the filling of roast fowl, or mix with breadcrumbs, well seasoned and moistened, brown in butter, and serve with the meat.

Pigeons should be roasted in a quick oven. Large pigeons will roast in an hour; a small one in half an hour.

Ducks will roast in half an hour; wild ducks in fifteen or twenty minutes. This time is for roasting rare.

An ordinary-sized goose will roast in one hour.

A large turkey will require three hours to roast. Use Cranberry sauce and current jelly with fowls, veal, ham and game.

A spoonful of vinegar put into the water in which fowls are boiled makes them tender. The garnishes for turkey and chicken are parsley, fried oysters, thin slices of ham, slices of lemon and fried sausage.

Roast Turkey.

(Marion Harland.)

After drawing the turkey, rinse out with several waters, and in next to the last mix a teaspoonful of soda. The inside of a fowl, especially if purchased in the market, is sometimes very sour, and imparts an unpleasant taste to the stuffing, if not to the inner part of the legs and side bones. The soda will act as a corrective, and is, moreover, very cleansing. Fill the body with this water, shake well, empty it out, and rinse with fair water. Then prepare a dressing of bread-crumbs, mix with butter, pepper, salt, thyme or sweet marjoram. You may, if you like, add the beaten yolks of two eggs. Mince a dozen oysters and stir into the dressing. The effect upon the turkey meat, particularly that of the breast, is very pleasant.

Stuff the craw with this, and tie a string tightly about the neck, to prevent the escape of the stuffing. Then fill the body of the turkey, and sew it up with strong thread. This and the neck-string are to be removed when the fowl is dished. In roasting, if your fire is brisk, allow about ten minutes to the pound; but it will depend very much upon the turkey's age whether this rule holds good. Dredge it with flour before roasting, and baste often; at first with butter and water, afterward with the gravy in the dripping-pan. If you lay the turkey in the pan, put in with it a teacup of hot water. Many roast always upon a grating placed on the top of the pan. In that case the boiling water steams the under part of the fowl, and prevents the skin from drying too fast, or cracking. Roast to a fine brown, and if it threatens to darken too rapidly, lay a sheet of white paper over it until the lower part is also done.

Stew the chopped giblets in just enough water to cover them, and when the turkey is lifted from the pan, add these with the water in which they were boiled, to the drippings; thicken with a spoonful of browned flour, wet with cold water to prevent lumping; boil up once, and pour into the gravy-boat.

Roast Turkey Without Stuffing.

(Mrs. C. W. F.)

The best authorities on cookery now agree that to stuff poultry is to ruin its flavor; and after once roasting a turkey without stuffing it, the housewife will ever after spare herself the labor of stuffing, which really does more harm than good. In dressing a turkey carefully remove every pin-feather, and singe off all hair.

Take out the crop through a cut made lengthwise in the skin of the neck, cut off the neck close to the body, fold down the neck skin on the breast, and secure it neatly with a small skewer. Open the body on the under side between the legs, and after loosening from the inside of the carcass the thin membrane which holds the intestines, take out the latter in a ball, being particular that they are not torn apart and that the gall, which lies under the liver, is not broken. If there is no mishap in removing the intestines, the inside of the bird will not need to be washed, but should merely be wiped out with a damp cloth. Poultry or game is never washed nowadays, unless it actually needs cleansing.

Carefully disengage the liver, gizzard and heart from the intestines, and set them aside to cook. Truss the turkey by folding the wings backward upon the back, really turning them against the back at the first joint. Secure the legs firmly and compactly to the sides by skewers, dust the turkey with pepper, and place strips of salt pork upon the breast. Set in a hot oven, and after thirty minutes diminish the heat. Roast without water, basting with the fat that cooks from the fowl; and allow twenty minutes cooking to each pound of turkey, not counting the first half hour. Sprinkle with salt when nearly done.

Place the heart, liver and gizzard on the fire in a stew-pan, and let them simmer, closely covered, for forty minutes; then remove, and chop finely. When the turkey is done, remove it to

French Plate Glass for Show Windows.
Crystal Plate Glass for dwellings.
Chances' Crystal Sheet Glass for dwellings.
French Double and Single Thick Glass for Dwellings.
American Double and Single Thick Glass for Dwellings.
Cathedral Glass, all tints, for Dwellings.
Enameled or Figured Glass for Doors, etc.
Plain Ground Glass for Offices, etc.
Ribbed Glass for Skylights.
Hammered Glass for Floors.
Cut and Embossed Glass for Doors.
Plain and Beveled Edge French Plate Mirrors.
Plain and Beveled Edge German Mirrors.
Glass Bent to order any Pattern.

CHAS. E. HODGKIN,

DEALER IN

Paints,

Oils,

Varnishes,

etc.

913 Seventh Street, N. W.

GLASS A SPECIALTY.

Washington, D. C.

DENHAM & WHITE,
GROCERIES,
Fresh Meats of All Kinds.
CHOICE BUTTER AND EGGS,
Cor. Eighth and S Streets, N. W.

BERNARD OSTMANN,
Choice Sugar Cured Bacon, Smoked Beef, Pork and Lard
DOVE BRAND HAMS COOKED AND RAW, TONGUES, &c.
Stall 190 Centre Market.   24 and 25 O St. Market.

serving dish, and set the roasting pan on top of the range in a gentle heat. Pour all but two tablespoonfuls of the oil, from the pan, add two tablespoonfuls of flour, and cook for three minutes. Then add the water in which the giblets were cooked, stir constantly, and pour in more water until the gravy is of the desired thickness. Add salt and pepper, if needed, and the chopped giblets, and serve in a gravy boat.

Chicken Pie.

(Mrs. D. W. Peetrey.)

One quart flour, 3 teaspoons of baking powder, 1 teacup of lard and butter, mixed, rub well together and moisten with cold water, enough to roll. Line the sides of the baking dish, with dough one quarter of an inch in thickness. Place in the chicken, having been well cooked, boned and seasoned. Fill the dish half full of the broth, bits of butter and sprinkle *heavily* with flour. Put on the top crust, the edges laping under the sides. Cut several gashes to let the steam escape, and bake until brown, in a quick oven.

Chicken Pie a la Reine.

One half pound salt pork, ½ teaspoonful each celery, salt and thyme, 4 sprigs parsley, white pepper and salt to taste. Cut chicken up in small joints, the pork in neat scallops, stew gently in 1½ pints water, until nearly cooked. Line edge of pudding dish with paste, make layers of chicken, pork and seasonings, when used, sprinkle over the chopped parsley; fill with the gravy, cover, ornament, and wash over with milk; bake in steady oven 40 minutes.

Roast Chicken.

Singe and truss carefully. Broilers, as they are called, are better without stuffing, unless very large. Season with salt, put small bits of butter over meat and place in pan with a little water; baste occasionally and dredge with flour before taking from oven. A spring chicken cooked in any style is not to be despised. But a well-known epicure once said:

"To roast spring chicken is to spoil it
Just split-down the back and broil it."

Chicken Pie with Oysters.

(Mrs. Parker.)

Boil a good sized chicken until tender, drain off the liquor from quart of oysters. Line the sides and bottom of a large, round pan with crust, put in a layer of oysters and a layer of chicken until the pan is full. Season with pepper, salt, bits of Cottolene and the oyster liquor, add some of the chicken liquor. Cover with crust and bake. Serve with sliced lemon.

Chicken a la Terrapin.

(Miss Helen L. Johnson.)

Make a rice border, as follows: Wipe $1\frac{1}{2}$ cups of rice on a soft towel. Cover with 1 quart of boiling stock and boil for 20 minutes. Then stand at the back of the stove for 15 minutes. Drain if necessary; season; press into a well greased border mold. Bake in a moderate oven for 20 minutes. Turn out of the mold.

While the rice is baking, prepare the chicken as follows: Take 1 pint of chicken meat. Add to it 2 tablespoonfuls of butter, rubbed smooth with 1 of flour. Stand over a moderate fire until heated, and add $\frac{1}{2}$ cup of cream, the whites of 2 hard boiled eggs mashed through a sieve; add to the yolks mashed and rubbed to a paste, 2 tablespoonfuls of cream. Stir this into the chicken, and let it come to boiling point. Season with salt, pepper and 1 tablespoonful of parsley chopped fine. Put in the centre of the border mold, and serve on a circular platter.

Smothered Chicken.

Cut up chicken for fricassee, wash and let stand in cold water a little while. Drain, season, dredge with flour, and put in dripping pan not quite covered with water. Dot with bits of butter. Cover closely and bake until tender. When done, take from pan and make a gravy.

Yankee Potpie.

(Mrs. C. W. F.)

Stew one chicken until tender and make a gravy with it as for fricassee. Take some fresh baking-powder biscuit, break them open and spread on a platter crust side down, and when ready to serve, pour over the chicken and gravy.

Pressed Chicken.

(Mrs. Parker.)

Take a large chicken, boil in very little water. When done, take the meat from the bones, remove the skin, chop and season. Press into a large bowl, add the liquor and put on a weight. When cold cut in slices and eat with sliced lemon or cucumber pickle.

Virginia Fried Chicken.

(Mrs. John Patterson.)

Dice and fry ½ pound of salt pork until it is well rendered. Cut up a young chicken, soak for half an hour in salt and water, wipe dry, season with pepper, roll in flour, and fry in hot fat until each piece is of a rich brown color. Take up and set aside in a warming closet. Pour into the gravy 1 cupful of milk —half cream is better; thicken with 1 spoonful of flour, and add 1 spoonful of butter and chopped parsley; boil up and pour over the hot chicken, or, if preferred, serve without the cream gravy, with bunches of fried parsley. Plain boiled rice should accompany this.

Pilaff of Chicken.

One small chicken, ½ cup rice, 1 teaspoonful salt.

Cut up the chicken the same as for a fricassee. Put in a stew

R. M. FROST,

DEALER IN

All Kinds of Salt Water Oysters,

FAMILIES, CLUBS, HOTELS AND PARTIES,

Served at Short Notice in Large or Small Quautities
with the Finest Select Stock.

ORDERS BY POSTAL RECEIVE PROMPT ATTENTION.

1500 8th St. N, W.

JOHN F. WEYRICK,
Stall 46 and 47 O St. Market N. W.
DEALER IN
First Class Beef, Lamb and Veal.
ORDERS PROMPTLY FILLED.

Open Monday, Wednesday and Friday mornings—
and Saturday afternoons.

GEORGE A. JORDAN,
REAL * ESTATE * BROKER,
No. 1417 F Street Northwest,
WASHINGTON, D. C.

pan, half cover it with water boiling, and set it on a moderate fire to simmer. Now wash the rice, add it to the chicken and the salt, and let all simmer until the chicken is tender. Make a tomato sauce. Dish the chicken and rice together, and pour over it the tomato sauce. This dish is very nice made from cold pieces of chicken or mutton.

Braised Duck.

Before trussing the duck as if for roasting, place inside it 2 chopped onions. Mix with them 1 dessertspoonful of sage, 1 tablespoonful of bread crumbs and pepper and salt. Fasten securely. Put an ounce of butter into a saucepan and fry the duck until it is nicely browned. Then put in the stew pan gravy to half cover the duck, with an onion cut in slices. Simmer for three-quarters of an hour. Take up the duck and keep it hot, while you strain and take the grease off the gravy. Boil the gravy until reduced one-half. Return the duck to the gravy and keep hot for a quarter of an hour. Serve with a puree of peas.

Wild Ducks Roasted.

(Mrs. Owens.)

Prepare for roasting the same as any fowl. Parboil for 15 minutes with an onion in the water, and the strong fishy flavor that is sometimes so disagreeable in wild ducks will have disappeared. A carrot will answer the same purpose. Stuff with bread crumbs, a minced onion, season with pepper, salt and sage, and roast until tender. Use butter plentifully in basting. A half hour will suffice for young ducks.

Stewed Pigeons.

Slice 6 onions and fry in butter a nice brown, clean pigeons whole; put in each a little salt, pepper and parsley; take the onions from the butter, fry the birds a nice brown, add water and the onions, thicken and stew them about one and a half hours.

Quail.

Split them open at the back and broil them; the inside must invariably be broiled first. Serve on toast.

Curried Rabbit.

(S. C. B.)

Boil a pound of pickled pork for three-quarters of an hour, with three onions, a sprig of thyme and 1 quart of water. Put in the rabbit and boil gently for half an hour. Take up the rabbit and pork. Cut up the former into joints, and the pork in neat slices. Put back into the liquor the head, neck, liver and bits of rabbit left with the bones and trimmings of the pork, and let boil for an hour; then strain and skim the liquor free from fat. Reduce to one-half by boiling without the lid; put in the pork and rabbit, and allow them to simmer gently half an hour. Rub the onions to a pulp, add them to 1 gill of milk or cream, 1 tablespoonful of flour, 1 teaspoonful of curry powder and 1 teaspoonful of curry paste. Put this to the gravy; stir over the fire until it has thickened, and serve with well-boiled rice on a separate dish.

Squirrel Pie.

(Mrs. Owens.)

Clean one pair of squirrels and cut into small pieces. Wipe off with a damp cloth. Put into a stew pan with two slices of salt pork, and water to nearly cover. Cook until half done. Season it well and thicken the gravy. Pour into a deep dish, cover with pie-crust, and bake 30 minutes. Squirrels may be fried, broiled, or stewed, like chickens or rabbits.

Woodcock.

(Mrs. Owens.)

Many excellent cooks do not draw them, asserting that the trail should be left in, even by those who do not like it, and removed after it is served. They claim that the flavor of the bird is much impaired if the trail is taken out before cooking. It looks rather plausible, as they are said to live by suction, have no crop, and a stomach only the size of a bullet. The trail, head, and neck are regarded as great delicacies by epicures. For my own eating, I could not cook them without drawing.

Neck of Venison.

(S. L. B.)

Remove the bones, roll up the meat and tie tightly. Wrap the meat thus prepared in buttered paper. Put in a pan and baste frequently. An hour and a half will cook it. Remove the paper sprinkle pepper and salt over the meat, brown with butter. Fry the venison bones with two sliced onions, some gravy and a bacon bone or two, and make a rich gravy. Another sauce is made by dissolving a little currant jelly in the sauce, adding a lump of butter, a few drops of Chili vinegar and a glass of port wine.

Dressing for Broiled Game.

(Miss Wister.)

Mix an ounce of butter with about a teaspoonful of unmade mustard, salt, a dust of cayenne and a few drops of vinegar, or, if preferred, lemon juice. Score the flesh pretty deeply, coat it thickly with the above mixture and broil over a clear fire.

Potato Stuffing for Poultry and Game.

(Miss Wister.)

Potato stuffing may be used for any fowl, though it is better for ducks and geese. Take about 2 cups of mashed potatoes, 1 teaspoonful of onion juice or 2 spoonfuls of fine chopped onion, ½ cupful of milk or cream, 1 tablespoonful of butter, black pepper, salt, tablespoonful of chopped parsley; many like yolk of egg, about 2 to the above quantity; mix and beat well.

THE MONUMENTAL,

◎—Fashion Leaders in Fine Millinery—◎
AT POPULAR PRICES.

We keep constantly on hand a fine assortment of Ladies' and Childrens' trimmed and untrimmed Hats and Millinery novelties, also fine assortment of hosiery, Mens' Underwear, Handkerchiefs and Umbrellas.

939 F ST., N. W.

MRS. A. T. WHITING,
DEALER IN FINE MILLINERY.

Hats and Bonnets Bleached and Pressed in the Latest Styles.

No. 518 TENTH STREET, N. W.

S. Oppenheimer & Bro.,

HOLIDAY GOODS OF ALL KINDS AT AUCTION PRICES.

514, 9th St. N. W.

AGENTS FOR THE New Home Sewing Machine.

Preparing Frogs.

In preparing frogs for the table use only the hind quarters; wash in warm water, then soak in vinegar and salt for an hour; scald them and remove the skin; wipe dry and fry in butter.

MEMORANDA.

MEMORANDA.

Coal! Coal!! Coal!!!

If You Want the best Coal mined, free from dirt, trash and mineral impurities, at the lowest prices consistent with the best service, and, especially, if you want PROTECTION AGAINST SCARCITY OF COAL resulting from Strikes or insufficient transportation facilities, then

Take This Advice:

Avoid new, upstart firms with no capital or facilities, and whose stock in trade consists of high-sounding titles like **"We, Us, & Co."** Such a firm cannot give you the best service, and, being dependent on small consignments by railroad, it can furnish you no protection AGAINST SCARCITY.

CHOOSE

AN OLD, LARGE AND RELIABLE FIRM OF ESTABLISHED REPUTATION. Such a firm is that of

V. BALDWIN JOHNSON,

one of the largest dealers in the District of Columbia, and with more coal UNDER COVER than any other dealer in the city.

YARDS:

1101 Rhode Island Ave., N. W.
511 A Street, N. E.
519 Four-and-a-half St., S. W.

VEGETABLES.

"*Captus Nidore Culinæ.*"

Boil fresh, young vegetables in hard water; a little salt will harden the water at once.

Boil dried vegetables in soft water; a little baking soda will soften water, and is useful in freshening and making tender green vegetables that are a little old or not wholly fresh. A little sugar is an improvement to beets, turnips and squash.

Cabbage, turnips, carrots, parsnips and beets are good boiled with fresh meats. When vegetables are served with salt meats, they are good boiled in the liquor in which the meat has been cooked; take out the meat when done; then cook the vegetables.

Underdone vegetables are unpardonable.

Boil onions, medium size, one hour; green corn, twenty to twenty-five minutes; peas and asparagus, twenty to twenty-five minutes; potatoes half an hour; if very small, less time; cabbage and cauliflower, twenty-five mintues to half an hour; carrots and turnips, forty-five minutes when young; one hour in winter; Lima beans, if young, half an hour; old, forty-five minutes; beets, one hour in summer, an hour and a half or even 2 hours, if large, in winter; string beans, if slit or sliced and thin, half an hour; if only snapped, forty-five minutes. Regulate this time always by the time the meat will be done.

Vegetable oysters are good with every kind of meat. Beets, peas and beans with boiled or roast meats. Carrots, parsnips, turnips, greens and cabbage are eaten with boiled meats. Mashed turnips, onions and apple sauce with roast pork. Tomatoes with every kind of meat. If sweet potatoes are lacking flavor, place them in the sun for a few days—a week, when they will have their natural flavor.

Baked Potatoes.

Time, 1 hour. Take as many large potatoes as you wish, wash clean, then wipe dry, put them into quick oven for 1 hour. Serve them in napkin, with cold butter, pepper and salt.

Saratoga Potatoes.

(Mrs. Owens.)

Peel and slice thin into cold water. Drain well, and dry in a towel. Fry a few at a time in boiling Cottolene. Salt as you take them out, and lay them on coarse brown paper for a short time. They are very nice cold for lunch, or to take to picnics.

Lyonnaise Potatoes.

(Mrs. Owens.)

Boil, peel and slice 6 potatoes. Put a sliced onion into a hot buttered frying-pan. When a little brown, put in the potatoes, Season, and when a golden brown, sprinkle over them a tablespoon chopped parsley. A combination of onion and parsley always means Lyonnaise.

Scalloped Potatoes.

Butter a baking dish, pare potatoes and slice thin, put in dish a layer of potatoes, and sprinkle with salt, pepper and a little butter; then another layer of potatoes, etc., until dish is nearly full. Then fill with milk or cream. Bake one hour and a half.

Roasted Potatoes with Beef.

(Mrs. John Patterson.)

Pare the potatoes and place in the pan on the rack with the meat, basting when you do the beef. They will be nicely browned, and mealy when the meat is done.

Potato Puff.

(Marion Harland.)

Take 2 cupfuls of cold mashed potato, and stir into it 6 teaspoonfuls of melted Cottolene, beating to a white cream before adding anything else. Then put with this 2 eggs whipped very light and 1 teacupful of cream or milk, salting to taste. Beat all well, pour into a deep dish, and bake in a quick oven until it is nicely browned. If properly mixed, it will come out of the oven light, puffy and delectable.

Potato Croquettes.

(Mrs. E. C. Bixby.)

Pare, boil, and mash 6 good-sized potatoes. Add 1 tablespoonful of butter, ⅔ of a cupful of hot cream or milk, the whites of 2 eggs well beaten, salt and pepper to taste. When cool enough to handle, work into shape, roll in egg and bread crumbs, and fry in hot lard.

Baked Mushrooms.

Place some large flat ones, nicely cleaned and trimmed, on thin slices of well buttered toast, putting a little piece of butter in each, as also a pinch of pepper and salt; lay them on a baking tray and cover them carefully; heap the hot ashes upon them, and let them bake on the hearth for fifteen or twenty minutes.

Fried Mushrooms.

When peeled put them into hot butter and let them heat thoroughly through—too much cooking toughens them; season well with butter, pepper and salt; serve on buttered toast; a teaspoonful of wine or vinegar on each mushroom is a choice method.

Broiled Mushrooms.

Choose the largest sort, lay them on a small gridiron over bright

BELMONT DAIRY,

1804 Fourteenth St., N. W. E. P. THOMAS, Proprietor.

MILK, CREAM AND BUTTER,

Home-Made Sausage, Eggs, Poultry, Potatoes.

PURITY AND FRESHNESS GUARANTEED.

All Fuel Kept Under Cover.

M. SELLS,

—DEALER IN—

Coal, Wood and Coke,

1840 FOURTEENTH STREET, NORTHWEST,

Telephone Call, 887-2.

TERMS CASH.

UNITED STATES CLAIM AGENCY.
W. W. CURRY, Attorney,
Washington, D. C.

PATENTS.

A PATENT is a grant by the Government for a specified term of years, of the exclusive right to make, use, and sell the invention throughout the country. YOU CAN PATENT any new and useful art, machine, manufacture, or composition of matter; or any new and useful improvement; or any new and useful combination of parts. Ideas are not patentable, only the *inventions* in which they are embodied.

If you have anything to patent, write me about it.

coals, the stalk upward; broil quickly, and serve with butter, pepper and put salt over.

Stewed Mushrooms.

Let them lie in salt and water 1 hour, then cover with fresh water and stew until tender; season with butter, salt and pepper; cream, if you wish.

Fried Tomatoes.

(Miss Mary Worick.)

Cut tomatoes in slices without skinning; pepper and salt them; then sprinkle a little flour over them and fry in butter until brown. Put them on a hot platter and pour milk or cream into the butter and juice. When boiling hot pour over tomatoes.

Stuffed Tomatoes.

(Mrs. C. W. F.)

Twelve large smooth tomatoes, 1 teaspoonful of salt, a little pepper, 1 tablespoonful of butter, 1 of sugar, 1 cupful of bread crumbs, 1 teaspoonful of onion juice. Arrange the tomatoes in a baking pan. Cut a thin slice from the smooth end of each. With a small spoon scoop out as much of the pulp and juice as possible without injuring the shape. When all have been treated in this way, mix the pulp and juice with the other ingredients, and fill the tomatoes with this mixture. Put on the tops and bake slowly three quarters of an hour. Slide the cake turner under the tomatoes and lift gently onto a flat dish. Garnish with parsley and serve.

Yum-Yum.

(Miss Wister.)

Baked tomatoes, partly stuffed with crab meat, are a new delicacy, and a sandwich made of one slice of a large, ripe, juicy tomato with a layer of crab meat, cooked Creole style, is said to be delicious.

Onions Stuffed With Kidneys.

Peel six large onions, cut about an inch from the top of each, scoop out the center so as to admit a piece of kidney about an inch square, lay the onions in a saucepan, season them with salt and pepper, cover them with cold gravy or broth of any kind, and stew them gently for 2 hours; take them up carefully without breaking them and serve them hot. The pieces cut from them should be chopped fine, mixed with any bits of kidney remaining from the dish, mixed with double their quantity of cold chopped potatoes, or bread soaked in cold water, and fried for a supper dish. Any kind of kidneys can be used.

Boiled Onions.

Choose small onions, unless they are too tiny, allow one for each guest. Place them on the stove in hot water, and let them simmer gently for ten minutes; then change the water, and cook them until tender. Make a cream sauce of the following: 1½ pint of milk, 1 tablespoonful of butter, 2 tablespoonfuls of flour, ½ teaspoonful of salt. Wet the flour with some of the milk, and add it to the balance of the milk when the latter is heated to the boiling point. Stir the sauce until it is creamy, and then add the salt and butter. Place the onions in the serving dish, pour over them the cream sauce, add a dusting of pepper, and serve.

Fried Onions.

Peel (holding onions and hands under water to prevent tears), wash and cut crosswise so as to form undivided rings. Flour them, fry 5 or 6 minutes. Drain, sprinkle with salt and pepper, serve with beefsteak.

Cauliflower au Parmesan.

Boil a fine, firm head of cauliflower in boiling salted water for twenty minutes. While boiling prepare a cream sauce with a tablespoonful of butter melted without browning, 1 tablespoonful of flour; stir until smooth. Add one cup of cream, and stir until it thickens. Add 2 tablespoonfuls of Parmesan cheese, and a dash of white pepper. Grease a baking dish; cut the cauliflower in pieces; put a layer, first of cauliflower, then of the sauce, and continue until all is used. Sprinkle the top with bread crumbs and brown in a quick oven.

Boiled Cauliflower.

Cut off the leaves, also stalk close to the bottom of the flowers. Place for a few moments in cold water, then put in salted boiling water and cook until tender. A piece of coarse netting tied about it will prevent its breaking. Serve hot with a little drawn butter poured over it, and each person eating with a little vinegar if they desire.

Turnips a la Creme.

Cut peeled turnips into half inch dice, boil in salted water and drain, pour over a cream sauce made of 1 cup hot milk poured gradually over 1 tablespoonful each butter and flour rubbed together. Salt and pepper.

Macaroni, with Cheese.

(Juliet Corson.)

The importance of this article of food is beginning to be realized in this country, and now it remains only to learn how to cook it palatably. Carefully follow the directions given and you cannot fail to produce a delicious dish of macaroni, fit for the most finished epicure's taste.

First of all, remember that good macaroni is always of a yellowish color. That which has a white, blanched appearance is decidedly inferior, You can buy the genuine Italian macaroni at the Italian stores generally to be found in our large cities, or from regular grocers or dealers in general stores. It costs in New York fifteen cents a pound. One pound after being properly boiled is increased in quantity about fourfold. To boil it

The Warren Shoe House,

GEO. W. RICH,

919 F Street, Northwest,

✹ WASHINGTON, D. C. ✹

The People's Resort for Genuine Bargains.

E. Kurtz Johnson. Telephone Call 762-2. Richard A. Johnson.

JOHNSON BROTHERS,
✹ Coal, Coke and Wood, ✹

MAIN OFFICE, 1206 F STREET, N. W.

BRANCHES:

1515 Seventh Street, N. W. Third and K Streets, N. W.
First and M Streets, N. E. Twelfth and Water Streets, N. W.

WHARVES AND RAILROAD YARDS:

Foot of Twelfth Street, S. W. First and M Streets, N. E.

Supply More Families with Fuel than Any One Firm
in the United States.

NO CHARGE FOR STORING COAL WITH "CHUTE" WAGON.

properly have a large pot or saucepan two-thirds full of water on the fire, put a level tablespoonful of salt into it to every quart of water, and when it is boiling fast throw into it the macaroni, wiped with a clean dry cloth, but not washed. Let it boil until it yields easily to pressure between the fingers; then drain it in a colander, and rinse it thoroughly in cold water; let it stand in cold water until you are ready to finish it according to any given recipe. The following is an excellent one.

Put into a saucepan one ounce each of butter and flour, and stir them together over the fire until they form a smooth, thick paste. Meantime put a little milk and water (about a gill of each) to boil, and when they are at the boiling point pour them gradually into the butter and flour, and stir altogether with an egg-whip.

If thicker than pudding sauce add a little boiling water; when the sauce has boiled up once, season it to taste with pepper, salt and just a grating of nutmeg. It is then ready for the macaroni, which must be put in it to be heated; while this is heating grate two ounces of hard, dry cheese, and mix it with the macaroni, which can be served as soon as it is hot. Or you can make it a little nicer by putting it on a shallow metal dish, sprinkling it well with bread or cracker crumbs, putting a few bits of butter on top of it and browning it in the oven. Macaroni prepared in this way is one of the most palatable of dishes, as well as one of the most wholesome and economical of foods.

Hot Slaw.

(Mrs. Parker.)

Chop fine and sprinkle over with flour. Put a small piece of butter in the oven to melt. Salt and pepper the cabbage, and put in the pan with the butter. Mix ½ a teacupful of cream, 1 egg, 1 tablespoonful of mustard, 1 teaspoonful of sugar, and heat thoroughly. Serve warm.

Hubbard Squash.

Split the squash in ½, remove the seeds, place in a baking tin, and bake for one hour. Remove from the oven, scrape the soft pulp from the shell, season well with butter, salt and pepper, and serve very hot.

Vegetable Oysters.

Cut them in thin slices, boil in clear water until soft, then pick a little codfish fine and add to the oysters, boil all together a few minutes, then season the same as oysters. Eat with crackers.

Hulled Corn.

One quart of corn, put to soak at night in warm water; in the morning change the water to enough to boil it in, putting in a rounding teaspoonful of soda and boil till it will hull. Rinse as usual.

Succotash.

Boil 1 quart lima or string beans until tender, cut down the middle the grains of 1 dozen ears corn, and scrape. Drain off water from beans, add the corn, season with salt, pepper and a good lump of butter. If too dry add a little cream or milk. Cook twenty minutes after adding the corn.

Stewed Celery.

(Mrs. Parker.)

Clean the heads, take off the coarse, outer leaves. Cut in small pieces and stew. When tender, add cream, butter, and a little flour. Season to taste.

Celery.

This is no longer served in a high glass, but in a low, flat dish that is much more elegant in appearance. Celery stalks should be scrubbed lengthwise with a small brush kept for the purpose, and should then be well rinsed and all rusty lines scraped off with a silver knife. The simple dishes of a meal are the ones to be most watchful of, and one of these is celery, which is too often only half cleansed, and served in anything but an appetizing manner.

Beets.

Do not break the skins in washing or they will loose their color in cooking. Boil one hour in hot, slightly salt water. Rub off the skins, split in half, dish, and pour on them a boiling mixture of 1 tablespoonful of melted butter, 1 of vinegar and a little pepper and salt. Serve *very* hot.

Stewed Spinach.

Dress in the ordinary way, and then chop fine and then rub through a wire sieve; put into a stew pan on the fire with some fresh butter, salt, white pepper, and grated nutmeg; stir, and add a piece of fiare, a little more butter, and mix well; then serve with sippets, fried in butter.

Parsnips (Fried.)

(M. C. H.)

Wash, scrape, clean and boil until quite tender. Drain; slice the long way of the parsnips, and fry in good dripping. Serve hot; lay them on a clean napkin to absorb the grease. They are very nice cooked this way.

Egg Plant.

Peel and cut in thin slices across the egg plant. Lay for half an hour in salt and water. Before cooking lay in flour, and fry in lard until well browned. Eat very hot.

Cabbages Cooked in Cream.

Take 2 quarts of chopped cabbage, boil until tender and the water is nearly gone; then pour in ⅔ of a cup of cream, with salt and pepper to the taste; boil fifteen minutes, and serve; or, instead of the cream use vinegar, with butter the size of a walnut, and you have "hot slaw."

J. WILLIAM LEE,

Successor to

❈ HENRY LEE'S SONS, ❈

UNDERTAKER,

332 Penna. Avenue,

Between 3d and 4½ Streets, N. W.

BRANCH OFFICE:

498 Maryland Avenue, S. W.

WEDDING
CAKES,
SMALL
CAKES.

BLOCK
ICE CREAM
FOR CHURCHES,
ETC.

GO TO

F. FREUND,

815 Tenth St., N. W.

FOR ICE CREAM,

WATER ICES

AND CAKES.

SPECIAL RATES FURNISHED TO CHURCHES, CLUBS, LODGES, ETC.

815 Tenth St., N. W.

TELEPHONE 796.

Green Corn Patties.

One pint of grated corn, 1 egg, 1 spoonful of flour, 1 spoonful of sweet milk, pepper and salt. Fry on griddle, with equal parts of butter and lard.

Fried Egg Plant.

Peel egg plants, slice thin, sprinkle little salt over them, and let them remain ½ an hour; wipe slices dry, dip them into beaten yolk of egg, then into grated cracker, fry them light brown in boiling lard, seasoning slightly with pepper while they are cooking. Another way is to parboil the egg plants, after they are peeled, in water with a little salt, then slice thin, dust them with corn meal, flour, or corn starch, and fry brown.

Green Peas.

Shell the peas and wash well in cold water. Cook in boiling water for 25 minutes. A lump of sugar will be a pleasant addition to market peas. Drain well; stir in a great lump of butter, and pepper and salt. Serve hot.

Boiled Asparagus.
(Miss Wister.)

Cut and peel the tough ends of the asparagus, tie it in little bunches and let it remain in cold water until ready to cook. Then put in a kettle of salted boiling water, and let it boil twenty-five minutes. Toast some slices of bread, butter it and place it on a heated plate. Drain the asparagus, cut the strings, lay it on the toast and pour over it a sauce made by stirring 1 tablespoonful of flour into 1 tablespoonful of melted butter; when smooth add some of the water in which the asparagus was cooked and boil, seasoning with salt and pepper.

Fried Apples.
(Miss Wister.)

Peel and cut into eighths, taking out the seeds and cores carefully from each piece; heat some Cottolene in a frying pan, coat the apples lightly with flour and fry to a pale brown; drain off the fat from each slice, sprinkle with sugar and pile on a hot dish; if you like you may mix a little cinnamon with the sugar; use only tart apples for frying. Send around slices of buttered brown bread with them.

Boston Baked Beans.

(Mrs. A. G. Rogers.)

One quart white beans soaked over night in cold water. In morning parboil until you can take beans in a spoon and blow off the skin. Add piece soda size of a pea, drain off that water and add more boiling water. Continue to boil until soft, then put in a bean pot with a pound of salt pork, streaked fat and lean, gash the pork. Add 2 teaspoons each of molasses, sugar and mustard. Put pork in middle of beans, cover all with water. Bake slowly all day.

Butter or Lima Beans.

(Mrs. C. W. F.)

One quart lima' beans, boil slowly 2 hours in enough salted water to cover them, when soft and tender add 1 cup sweet cream, butter size walnut, dash of pepper. Thicken with flour wet up with water, let all boil up and serve hot.

MEMORANDA.

L. P. HOSFORD, M. D.　　　MISS M. E. BARTLETT,
　　　　　　　　　　　　　　　　　Electrician.

HOSFORD

Electric, Medicated and Vapor Baths.

Successfully treat Nervous Prostration, Torpid Liver, Lumbago, Rhumatism Paralysis and Catarrh, Malaria and Spinal Irritation.

Circulation stimulated and equalized Skin cleaned, Perspiration profuse. No shock to the most sensitive system.

Complexion Steaming and Facial Massage by a Thorough Expert.

◆REFERENCES AND PAMPHLET FURNISHED ON APPLICATION.◆

Baths administered and Cabinets for Sale at

918 H ST., N. W.　　　　　　　WASHINGTON, D. C.

SALADS.

"To make a perfect salad there should be a spendthrift for oil, a miser for vinegar, a wise man for salt, and a madcap to stir the ingredients up and mix them well together.—SPANISH PROVERB.

Salads are very suitable for warm weather, or any weather, and there are few vegetables and few varieties of fish, flesh and fowl from which a salad cannot be made.

To have your vegetables crisp and fresh, soak them in cold water for an hour, dry them with a soft towel, and keep them in a cool place till you use them. Meats and fish may be cut up, and kept in a cool place, but do not mix the dressing with any salad until you are ready to serve. Any of the dressings given make good salads. Lettuce is the best vegetable for meat and fish salads, but other "greens" may be used. Some think meat and fish salads improved if seasoned with a little French dressing before made up with mayonnaise dressing. The hostess always serves the soup, salad and dessert, and it is now customary for her to make the dressing for a salad at table in the presence of her guests.

Cabbage Salad.

(Mrs. J. W. Webb.)

Shred or chop a head of white cabbage and pour over it the following: Dressing yolk of 1 egg, 1 saltspoon salt, 1 teaspoonful mustard, 1 tablespoonful sugar, 1 tablespoonful vinegar. Rub well together, add 3 tablespoonfuls milk, and lump of butter size of an egg. Place in double boiler stirring constantly until thick.

Chicken Salad.
(Mrs. Parloa.)

One quart chicken meat; 3 tablespoonfuls vinegar; 1 tablespoonful oil; 1 generous teaspoonful salt; ½ teaspoonful pepper; 1 pint celery; mayonnaise dressing.

Free cold cooked chicken of skin, fat and bones, and cut it in cubes. Put 1 quart of the meat in a bowl with a marinade made by mixing vinegar, oil, salt and pepper. Stir well, and place in the refrigerator for 1 hour or longer.

Cut in thin slices enough of the white, tender part of celery to make a generous pint. Wash this in cold water, and put it in the refrigerator with pieces of ice on top. At serving time remove the ice, and drain all the water from the celery. Mix the celery with the chicken, and add ½ a pint of mayonnaise dressing. Arrange the salad in a bowl or on a flat dish. Mask it with ½ a pint of mayonnaise, and garnish with some of the blanched celery leaves.

Cucumber and Onion Salad.

Pare cucumbers and lay in ice-water 1 hour; do same with onions in another bowl. Then slice them in proportion of 1 onion to 3 large cucumbers, arrange in salad bowl. Use the following:

Salad Dressing.
(Mrs. C. H. Ford.)

Beat the yolks of 2 raw eggs with the yolks of 2 eggs boiled hard, and mashed fine as possible; add gradually a tablespoon prepared mustard, 3 of melted butter, a little salt and pepper and vinegar to taste.

Egg Salad.
(Miss. Wister.)

Take as many eggs as needed, boil them until perfectly hard, almost half an hour. Take out the yolks carefully, chop the white very fine. Arrange lettuce leaves or cress on a dish, making nests of the whites of the eggs, and put one yolk in each nest; sprinkle dressing over the whole.

Fish Salad.

(Miss Wister.)

One can of salmon, or the same of any cold fish, either boiled or baked, and from which remove the skin and bones. Chop, when cold, 3 large boiled potatoes, and mix with the fish. Rub smooth the yolks of 3 hard boiled eggs, season with pepper, salt and mustard; add 2 tablespoonfuls of cream and 1 gill of vinegar; pour the dressing over the fish and potatoes.

Lettuce Dressing.

(Mrs. Currier.)

Yolk of 4 eggs, 1 cup milk, 1 cup vinegar, 4 tablespoonfuls melted butter or oil. Sugar to taste and cayenne pepper; ½ teaspoonful mustard.

Lobster Salad.

Cut the meat of 2 small lobsters into small pieces. Add a little of the fat and coral. Then season with salt and pepper, and pour over enough mayonnaise dressing to moisten well. Put in the middle of a platter, garnish with lettuce leaves, pour over the remainder of the dressing, and put slices of boiled egg, and olives over the top.

Oyster Salad.

Let fifty small oysters just come to a boil in their own liquor. Skim and strain. Season the oysters with 3 tablespoonfuls of vinegar, 1 of oil, ½ teaspoonful of salt, ⅛ teaspoonful of pepper, and place on ice for 2 hours. With a sharp knife cut up a pint of celery, using only the tender part, and when ready to serve, mix with the oysters, adding about ½ pint of mayonnaise dres-

JOHN R. WRIGHT,

Embalmer and Undertaker,

1337 TENTH ST., N. W.,

Telephone Call, 709. Washington, D. C.

Telephone Call 225-2.

G. Y. HANSELL,

DEALER IN

Foreign and Domestic Wall Papers,

INTERIOR DECORATOR,

No. 601 H Street, N. E.

W. D. CLARK. R. P. CLARK.

W. D. CLARK & CO.,

Dealer in First-Class Dry Goods,

No. 811 Market Space, Penna. Avenue,

WASHINGTON, D. C.

sing. Arrange in a salad dish. Pour over another ½ pint of dressing, and garnish with white celery leaves.

Potato Salad.

(Aunt Tee.)

Four large cold potatoes; 3 small onions; 1 large cucumber, add lettuce and celery according to taste and convenience, place on ice, and serve with the following *dressing*:—one or 2 eggs well beaten; 1 large teaspoonful butter; ½ teaspoonful mustard; ¼ teaspoonful black pepper; trifle cayenne; salt to taste; ½ cup vinegar, when ready for use, thin if desired.

Shrimp Salad.

(Mrs. M. C. Currier.)

Cut and peel fair raw tomatoes, removing the inside, fill with shrimps, put over a spoonful of mayonnaise dressing. Serve on lettuce leaves with radishes cut like tulips.

Sardine Salad.

For 1 large box of sardines, take 6 hard boiled eggs, drain off the oil from the fish, remove backbone, tail and skin, and mix thoroughly with the eggs, minced fine; season with pepper and salt. Serve plain, with vinegar, or mayonnaise dressing.

Red Vegetable Salad.

(Mrs. C. W. F.)

One pint of cold boiled potatoes, 1 pint of cold boiled beets, 1 pint of uncooked red cabbage, 6 tablespoonfuls of oil, 8 of red vinegar (that in which beets have been pickled), 2 teaspoonfuls of salt (unless the vegetables have been cooked in salted water), ½ a teaspoonful of pepper. Cut the potatoes in thin slices and the beets fine, and slice the cabbage as thin as possible. Mix all the ingredients. Let stand in a cold place one hour, then serve with dressing.

Tomato and Celery Salad.

(Miss Kate Curry.)

Scald and peel smooth, round tomatoes. Cut a slice off at the stem end and carefully remove the seeds. Place on ice until cold, then fill with celery cut into small pieces and moistened with mayonnaise. Serve each tomato on a crisp lettuce leaf.

Mayonnaise Dressing.

(J. F. B.)

Add to the yolk of 1 egg 1 teaspoonful of mustard, 1 of salt, 1 of sugar, a little pepper. Mix thoroughly. Then add a small cupful of oil, mixing it in drop by drop until it becomes like butter. Add about 4 teaspoonfuls of vinegar. When ready to use it, thin with a little condensed milk.

French Salad Dressing.

(J. F. B.)

Take the yolk of 1 egg; 6 tablespoonfuls of oil; 3 tablespoonfuls of vinegar, and a little salt. Shake together in a bottle until white. Pour over the lettuce.

MEMORANDA.

W. H. HOEKE,

Carpets, Furniture and Upholstery Goods,

801 Market Space, and 308 and 310 Eighth Streets.

John J. Costinett,

:::: ARMY AND NAVY :::: **Tailor,**

FASHIONABLE CIVILIAN DRESS,

624 14th Street, N. W.

Knights Templer Regalia.

Cleaning, Altering and Repairing.　　　　WASHINGTON, D. C.

HARTUNG'S DAIRY,
Prospect St., N. E.
MILK AND CREAM A SPECIALTY,
Delivery Twice Per Day.

Milk 8 cents per quart.　　　　Cream 12 cents per pint.
Orders by mail promptly attended to.

PICKLES AND MEAT SAUCES.

" Peter Piper picked a peck of pickled peppers."
" What is sauce for the Goose is sauce for the Gander."

Cucumber Pickles.
(Mrs. Webb.)

Two hundred small cucumbers; 15 small white onions; 1 handful horse-radish root cut small; 1 dozen small green peppers; put all in salt water and let stand over night; in the morning when you take out of salt water, add ½ oz. of each of the following ground spices:—cloves, cinnamon, all-spice, mace, celery seed, white mustard seed and a very little red pepper; 1 pound of brown sugar; also an oz. of tumeric. Put the pickles in a jar, and put spices on top and cover with cold sharp vinegar.

Hidgen Pickle.
(Mrs. H. E. W.)

One peck green tomatoes chopped finely; add 1 handful salt; drain three or four times; then add 2 heads of cabbage, 4 large onions, 6 green peppers, all chopped finely. Cover this with vinegar; let it boil five minutes; drain off the vinegar. Then take fresh vinegar enough to cover it. Put it all over the fire and scald, with 2 ounces whole cassia, 1 ounce cloves, 1 large tablespoonful mustard; and 1 pint of molasses. Stir well. When cold cover tightly in stone jars.

Chilli Sauce.

(Miss M. H. Gould.)

Thirty-six large ripe tomatoes, peel core and chop fine; 4 onions, 3 red and 3 green peppers, remove seed and chop fine; 3 tablespoonfuls salt, 2 cups vinegar, 1 cup sugar, 2 tablespoonfuls ground cinnamon, 1 tablespoonful cloves, 1 tablespoonful celery seed. Put all on except spices and boil until thick, add spices and boil for 20 minutes longer, then bottle or jar while hot.

Chow Chow.

(Mrs. A. E. Hoyle.)

One-half peck green tomatoes, 4 onions, 4 large peppers, 1 head cabbage. Chop fine and salt over night, then strain through coarse seive and with 1 quart vinegar, 1 cup sugar, ½ tablespoonful mustard, boil until tender, then add 1 teaspoonful ground cloves, 1 teaspoonful cinnamon, 1 teaspoonful allspice, 1 teaspoonful tumeric, ½ teaspoonful black pepper, and jar while hot.

Tomato Catsup.

(Mrs. Geo. Barnes.)

One and one-half pecks ripe tomatoes, boil and strain through a seive; add 3 tablespoonfuls salt, ½ pound brown sugar, 2 teaspoonfuls cloves, 2 of mustard, 1 of red pepper, 1 of celery seed; boil 1½ hours, then add 1 quart cider vinegar, boil another hour, bottle and seal.

Sweet Pickled Cantaloupe.

(Mrs. Keech.)

Nine pounds fruit; 3 pounds brown sugar; 1 quart vinegar; 1

teaspoonful cinnamon; 1 teaspoonful cloves; 1 teaspoonful mace; 2 teaspoonfuls celery seed.

Peach, Pear and Plum Pickles.

To every quart of vinegar add a pound of brown sugar, boil and skim. Wipe the fruit, stick three or four cloves in each. Boil in the vinegar, a few at a time, until tender. Skim them out, and cool. When all is done put in a jar, and turn the vinegar over them hot. Cinnamon and allspice may be added in the vinegar, if desired.

Spiced Damsons.

Seven pounds damson plums; 1 pound brown sugar; 1 and ½ pints of vinegar; 1 ounce cloves; 1 ounce cinnamon. Boil 4 hours, taking out the pits as they rise. Use either whole or ground spice.

Spiced Currants.

(Mrs. John Patterson.)

Five pounds currants, 4 pounds brown sugar, 2 tablespoonfuls cloves, 2 tablespoonfuls cinnamon, 1 pint vinegar; boil 2 hours or till quite thick.

Shirley Sauce, for Meats.

(Mrs. J. M. Welty.)

Eight large tomatoes, 4 large onions, 1 green pepper, 4 tart apples, 1 tablespoonful salt, 2 pints *brown* sugar, 1 quart of vinegar, 1 tablespoonful cloves, 1 tablespoonful cinnamon, 1 tablespoonful allspice. Hash all very fine and boil about an hour and a half.

Maitre d'Hotel Sauce.

(Mrs. Parker.)

Add to 1 teacupful of fresh made drawn butter, the juice of 1 small lemon, chopped parsley, minced onions and thyme, cayenne pepper and salt. Beat while simmering. Serve with meat or fish.

AGE PRINTING CO.,

BOOK AND JOB PRINTERS.

INVENTIVE AGE BUILDING.

COR. 8TH AND H STS., N. W.,

TELEPHONE, 1516.   WASHINGTON, D. C.

Have You Seen The

NEW HAMMOND TYPEWRITER?

It possesses all Old and many New advantages.

JOHN C. PARKER,

619 7th Street, N. W.

WELCOME FOOT BATH,

Why go with tired feet when by using the Welcome Foot Bath all soreness will be removed.

MRS. I. M. HOLLISTER, Sole Proprietor, Hartford, Conn.

For sale at Palais Royal, Bentley's Drug Store and Lansburgs.

AGENTS WANTED.

H. S. HAIGHT,

GROCER,

✸ Headquarters for Holiday Goods. ✸

Established 1876.   Cor. 11th and S Streets, N. W.

Oyster Sauce.

("Marion Harland.")

One pint oysters; half a lemon; 2 tablespoonfuls butter; 1 tablespoonful flour; 1 teacupful milk or cream; cayenne and nutmeg to taste.

Stew the oysters in their own liquor five minutes, and add the milk. When this boils, strain the liquor and return to the saucepan. Thicken with the flour when you have wet it with cold water; stir it well in; put in the butter, next the cayenne (if you like it), boil one minute; squeeze in the lemon juice, shake it around well, and pour out.

Or, drain the oysters dry without cooking at all; make the sauce with the liquor and other ingredients just named. Chop the raw oysters, and stir in when you do the butter; boil five minutes, and pour into the tureen. Some put in the oysters whole, considering that the sauce is handsomer than when they are chopped.

Oyster sauce is used for boiled halibut, cod, and other fish, for boiled turkey, chickens, and white meats generally.

Roman Sauce.

(Mrs. Parker.)

Put 1 teacupful of water and 1 of milk on the fire to scald; stir in a tablespoonful of flour and 3 well beaten eggs. Season with pepper and salt, 2 ounces of butter and a tablespoonful of vinegar. Boil 4 eggs, slice and lay over the dish. Serve with boiled tongue, beef, venison or fish.

Currant Sauce for Venison.

(Juliet Corson.)

Half an hour before the venison is done pick over an ounce of dried currants, wash them well, put them over the fire in half a pint of hot water, and boil them for fifteen minutes; then add to them 2 heaping tablespoonfuls of bread crumbs, 1 of butter, a palatable seasoning of salt and pepper, and 6 whole cloves, and boil the sauce gently; just before serving it add a glass of port wine.

Tomato Sauce.

(Mrs. Rorer.)

One pint of stewed tomatoes; 1 tablespoonful flour; 3 level teaspoonfuls Cottolene; 1 small onion; 1 bay leaf; 1 sprig parsley; 1 blade mace; salt and pepper to taste.

Put the tomatoes on the fire with the onion, bay leaf, parsley and mace, and simmer slowly for ten minues. Melt the Cottolene, add it to the flour; mix until smooth. Press the tomatoes through a seive, add them to the Cottolene and flour, stir continually until it boils, add salt and pepper, and it is ready to use.

This may be served with chops, fillet, or broiled steak.

English Sauce.

One tablespoonful of grated horse radish; 1 teaspoonful of made mustard; 4 tablespoonfuls of vinegar; 1 teaspoonful of powdered sugar. Blend together and serve immediately. For cold or hot roast beef.

Cranberry Sauce.

(Mrs. C. W. F.)

One quart of cranberries; 1 pint of boiling water; 2 cupfuls of sugar. Wash the berries carefully, place them in a granite kettle, pour over them the boiling water, and cook for seven minutes. Remove from the fire, pass through a colander, return to the kettle, add the sugar, cook for one minute, and turn out to cool.

Drawn Butter Sauce.

(Mrs. H. D. Bates.)

Put half a teacupful of butter in a saucepan and when melted add 2 tablespoonfuls of flour. Cook, but not brown, then add a pint of water and stir until smooth. Season with salt and pepper. This sauce is a nice addition to boiled or baked fish.

White Sauce.

One-third pint of cream; 2 ounces butter; 1 teaspoonful of flour; salt and pepper to taste; a litle lemon juice. Put the butter in a saucepan, dredge in the flour and the other ingredients; stir until they boil. The lemon is added when served. For boiled chicken.

Onion Sauce.

One-half pint of milk; 1 tablespoonful of flour, heat with a little butter; salt to taste. Chop 3 boiled onions, and then stir in. For roast mutton.

MEMORANDA.

THE UNIVERSAL COOK-BOOK.

MEMORANDA.

WESCOTT, WILCOX & HIESTON,

✸ Real Estate and Fire Insurance Agents, ✸

1907 Pennsylvania Ave., N. W.

WASHINGTON, D. C.

E. S. Wescott.   W. R. Wilcox.   W. Hieston.

RENT BRANCH,

✸ WESCOTT & WILCOX, ✸

Real Estate Agents,

RENTING A SPECIALTY,

1907 Pennsylvania Avenue, N. W.,

WASHINGTON, D. C.

E. S. WESCOTT.   W. R. WILCOX.

CHEESE.

Cheese is not found upon our tables often enough. It is an excellent digestant, when eaten moderately and is more nutritious than meats. The soft cheeses are richest and should be kept in a box in a cool dry place.

Cheese dishes prepared by these receipts may be served at lunch, dinner or tea with a salad.

Cheese Straws.

(Miss G. E. Merrill.)

Mix together 4 tablespoonfuls flour, pinch of salt, a very little cayenne pepper, and 3 ounces grated cheese. Add the beaten yolk of 1 egg, and then enough iced water to make a very stiff paste. Roll the paste on a board, into a sheet ⅛ inch thick. Cut the sheet into strips ⅛ inch wide, and 5 inches long; and bake them about ten minutes in a very hot oven.

Welsh Rarebit.

(Mrs. Rorer.)

Two cups grated cheese; 2 egg yolks; ½ cup milk; salt and cayenne to taste.

Toast carefully slices of bread with the crusts removed. While hot, butter them, and then plunge in a bowl of hot water. Place on a heated dish and stand in the oven to keep warm while you make the rarebit. Put the milk in a porcelain lined or granite saucepan; stand it over a moderate fire; when boiling hot, add the cheese; stir continually until the cheese is melted; add the salt, cayenne and yolks, and pour it over the toasted bread. If the rarebit is stringy and tough, it is the fault of the cheese not being rich enough to melt.

Old English dairy cheese makes the best Welsh rarebit.

Welsh Rarebits.

Put a little milk in a saucepan and set it on a moderate fire; cut up in slices some new cheese and put into the saucepan; stir the whole thoroughly until the cheese is melted and well mixed with the milk. Only a small portion of milk is necessary, say about one-eighth. Have some pieces of toast ready buttered, and on the bottom of a dish. When the cheese is thoroughly melted and mixed, pour it upon the toast and serve while hot.

Cheese Fondu.

Pour ½ a pint of boiling milk on the crumbs of a French roll, beat it up with a quarter of a pound of good cheese, grated, and the yolks of 2 well beaten eggs. Just as it is ready for the oven add the whites of 4 eggs, frothed. Bake in a quick oven in a deep dish. Serve immediately.

Cheese Souffle.

This dish must be sent to table direct from the oven in the pan in which it has been baked, as it falls if kept standing. Beat separately the whites and yolks of 2 eggs, add to the yolks 1 tablespoonful of sifted flour, 2 of grated cheese, a pinch of cayenne, one of salt, and 1 cup of milk; when well mixed add the whites beaten to a froth, and stir briskly, pour into a buttered shallow pan, and bake in a quick oven until a rich brown—about fifteen minutes.

Cottage Cheese.

(Mrs. C. W. F.)

Place 3 quarts bonny-clabber over the fire and when it curdles drain it through a seive. To this curd, add 1 cup sweet cream, or work in ½ cup butter, salt to taste and place in a cheese cloth, bag and hang up to dry, or press it into moulds.

Deviled Biscuit.

(Miss Parloa.)

One tablespoonful Parmesan cheese; 1 tablespoonful dry mustard; 1 tablespoonful olive oil; ½ teaspoonful salt; one-fifth teaspoonful cayenne; 2 tablespoonfuls milk.

Mix these ingredients together and spread the mixture lightly upon half a dozen soda biscuit, and toast over a hot fire. Serve immediately.

If objection be made to the use of oil, substitute a tablespoonful of melted butter. Only a delicate flavor is given to the biscuit by the ingredients named; and if a strong taste be desired, double the quantity of materials for the mixture.

Curried Cheese.

One dozen rolled crackers, ¼ pound grated cheese, salt, butter and curry powder to taste. Moisten with sweet milk, drop in hot gem-pan, bake 20 minutes. Serve with tomato sauce.

Snyder & Wood,

TAILORS,

1111 Pennsylvania Avenue, N. W.

A large stock of fine

WOOLENS

to select from.

Prices as Low as Consistent with First-Class Work.

SATISFACTION GUARANTEED.

Phone. 662.

EGGS.

Eggs half a day old are better for the cook than the "fresh laid egg."

Do not poach eggs that are not fresh. Serve bread with eggs. Eggs prepared in some of the receipts here given are served at lunch instead of soup.

Before beating eggs let them remain in cold water a little while.

Miss Helen Louise Johnson says: "There are several hundred ways of cooking eggs, this means largely that there are several hundred ways of making sauces to go over boiled eggs. There is more art in boiling an egg than is generally supposed. The albumen hardens at a low temperature, about 160 degrees, and the egg should be put in water but little hotter than this and allowed to stand till they are cooked. They are like coffee in this respect and should never be really 'boiled'."

Many physicians tell us, however, that an egg should be boiled from ½ to 1 hour to be the most easily digested. To tell good eggs from bad eggs—put them in water and the bad eggs will stand on end, the good ones will lie on the side. To keep eggs, put a 2 inch layer of salt in a stone jar, then a layer of fresh eggs —large end down—so on till the jar is full, with a layer of salt at top, cover and put in a cool place. Or the eggs may be rubbed over with lard and packed in oats or bran.

Poached Eggs.

Break the eggs, one at a time, into a saucer. Place water in a saucepan, salt it well, and when it is simmering, drop each egg lightly in, cooking but one egg at a time if the saucepan is small. More may be cooked at once by using a large frying-pan. The water should not be allowed to boil while the eggs are cooking, but should be kept just at the boiling point. With a spoon throw the water carefully on top of the egg to whiten it. The beauty of a poached egg lies in the yolk blushing through the white, which should be just sufficiently hardened to form a veil for the yolk. When cooked enough, take out the egg with a perforated ladle, trim the ragged edges, and slip the egg upon a small piece of thin, buttered toast. When all the eggs have been cooked and placed upon their separate pieces of toast, add to each a bit of butter and sprinkle with salt and pepper. Muffin rings are sometimes set in the water to give the eggs an even shape. If liked, sorrel may be sprinkled over the eggs.

Mrs. Hathaway's Omelet.

Three eggs, beaten separately, ½ cup milk, 1 teaspoonful corn starch, 1 tablespoonful melted butter added lastly. Put in hot skillet; cook and fold; chopped ham sprinkled on before folding improves it. Serve at once.

Bread Crumb Omelet.

(Mrs. Allyn.)

Two-thirds of a pint of fine dried bread crumbs, a teaspoonful of dried parsley, 1 spoonful of finely minced onions, 2 eggs, 1 pint of good sweet milk, 1 tablespoonful of butter and pepper and salt. Beat the eggs to a froth and mix with the milk. Then add the other ingredients. Butter a pan, put the crumbs in it, and pour the mixture over it. Bake to a light brown and serve at once.

French Economical Omlette.

(M. A. D.)

To 1 pint of boiling milk add 3 well beaten eggs, 1 teaspoonful corn starch and a pinch of salt. Turn into a pudding dish.

bake 20 minutes. To be eaten at *once*. A little dexterity must be used in mixing the eggs with the milk to prevent their separating.

Omelet with Oysters.

(Juliet Corson.)

Blanch 1 dozen small Blue Point oysters, by bringing them just to the boiling point in their own liquor, seasoned with a dust of cayenne, a saltspoonful of salt, and a grate of nutmeg; mix an omelet; place over the fire, and when it begins to cook at the edges, place the oysters, without any liquor, in its center, fold it together, and serve it hot at once.

Omelet with Cheese.

(Miss Wister.)

Four eggs; ½ cup milk; 1 teaspoonful flour; a little parsley; pepper and salt; ½ teacupful grated cheese; 1 tablespoonful Cottolene.

Beat the eggs very light and then add the other ingredients. Beat all well together and pour into a pan in which a large tablespoonful of Cottolene is heated. Let it cook till light brown, then fold it over and dish for the table. Shake the pan while the omelet is cooking. Must be eaten the instant it is removed from the pan.

Scrambled Eggs.

(Mrs. C. W. F.)

Take a small piece of butter and a little cream, warm in a frying pan. Break 6 eggs in it and stir until slightly cooked. Serve hot. Or scramble in pork drippings.

Tomato Omelet.

Make a plain omelet and pour tomato sauce around it just before serving.

NATIONAL CAPITAL ICE CO.

DEALER IN

Kennebec Ice,

BRANCH DEPOT:

O St. Market, Cor. 7th and O, N. W.

BUSINESS OFFICE AND DEPOT:

8th St. Wharf, S. W.

※ A NEW CYCLOPÆDIA ※
AT $\frac{1}{2}$ THE COST OF STANDARD EDITIONS,

AND **20** YEARS LATER.

JOHNSON'S, A new work from cover to cover. Under the control and supervision of those great Encyclopædic Publishers, The APPLETON'S, New York.

New matter, new maps, new illustrations, authoritive and scholarly in its character.

A new feature of this Cyclopædia is that the authentication of each article of importance is attested by the appending of the name of its author.

Thoroughly American in its character.

Adopted by all the Government and Scientific Departments.

No one, however busy, can afford to be a day without a good reference library.

Every one that reads, every one that mingles in society, is constantly meeting with allusions to subjects on which he needs and desires further information.

Send postal for specimen pages.

AGENTS WANTED.
D. APPLETON & CO.,

437 7th St., N. W.   WASHINGTON, D. C.

Curried Eggs.

(Miss Parloa.)

Six hard boiled eggs ; 1 cupful stock ; ½ cupful cream or milk; 1 teaspoonful chopped onion ; 3 tablespoonfuls butter ; 1 tablespoonful flour ; 1 teaspoonful curry powder ; salt and pepper to taste.

After cooking the onion and butter in a small frying pan for three minutes put in the flour and curry powder ; stir the liquid until it becomes smooth ; then add the stock and milk and some seasoning, and cook for ten minutes. Quarter the eggs and place them in a deep saucepan ; strain the sauce over them, and after simmering for three minutes, serve very hot, with toast.

The teaspoonful of curry powder gives a delicate flavor. More may be used if one desires.

Shirred or Baked Eggs.

(Miss Wister.)

Break each egg into a cup first, so that the yolk is not broken, put all into a buttered dish or saucepan in which they may be served ; put a little salt on each egg and bake in the oven until the whites are firm. Add a little butter and serve at once. Nice little egg shirrers, holding one or two eggs, are made for this purpose. The eggs are also very nice baked on slices of toast, or in any gravy you may have left from poultry.

Fricasseed Eggs.

(Miss Curry.)

Boil 6 eggs hard. When cold cut in slices about ⅛ inch thick and dip in beaten egg and then in cracker or bread crumbs. Fry in very hot oil or lard.

Pickled Eggs.

(Mrs. Owens.)

Boil eggs very hard and remove the shell. Take 1 teaspoonful each of cinnamon, allspice and mace; put in a little muslin bag in cold water; boil well, and if it boils away add enough to make ½ pint when the spices are taken out; add 1 pint of strong vinegar; pour over the eggs. If you want them colored put in some beet juice.

Eggs upon Toast.

(Mrs. Chas. Merrill.)

Put a good lump of butter into the frying pan. When it is hot stir in 4 or 5 well beaten eggs, with pepper, salt and a little parsley. Stir and toss for three minutes. Have ready to your hand some slices of buttered toast (cut round with a tin cake-cutter before they are toasted); spread thickly with ground or minced tongue, chicken or ham. Heap the stirred egg upon these in mounds, and set in a hot dish garnished with parsley and pickled beets.

Birds' Nest.

(Practical Housekeeping.)

Boil the eggs hard, remove shells, surround with forcemeat; fry or bake them till nicely browned, cut in halves and place in a dish with gravy.

MEMORANDA.

ELECTRIC MARKET,

L. R. Keech. J. H. Strong.

13TH AND W STREETS, N. W.

Dealer in Fine Groceries, Fresh Meats and Provisions.

TRY OUR ELECTRIC LIGHT FLOUR, EVERYBODY USES IT.

Coffee and Teas, Choice Syrups and Molasses, Fresh Country Eggs, Butter and Cheese from the Finest Dairies.

Salt Water Oysters, Fresh Fish.

Game of all Kinds in Season.

ALL STAPLE ARTICLES AT STAPLE PRICES.

Orders called for and promptly delivered.

KEECH & STRONG,

1235 W St., N. W., Cor. 13th.

BREAD and BREAKFAST CAKES, BISCUIT and ROLLS.

*"Here is bread which strengthens men's hearts,
And therefore is called, 'The Staff of life.'"*

Good bread makes the homliest meal acceptable and the coarsest fare appetizing, while the most luxurious table is not even tolerable without it. Light crisp rolls for breakfast, spongy, sweet bread for dinner, and flaky biscuit for supper, cover a multitude of culinary sins: and there is no one thing on which the health of a family so much depends, as the quality of its home-made loaves. Three things are indispensable to success in bread making: good flour, good yeast and good judgment. The use of Gluten Bread is very healthful. Graham flour is made both from white and amber wheat, the former possesses more delicacy, the latter more gluten. For family use the F S White Wheat Graham is superior. It makes healthful and nutritious bread particularly for those troubled with indigestion.

Bread and biscuit should rise in a moderately warm place. If too cold it will be heavy; if too hot it will be sour.

Should a batch of dough become sour, a teaspoonful of soda will help it, but this should be used only in an emergency.

To have your bread rise quickly, double the quantity of yeast, but watch it; do not let it sour.

Bread should rise to twice its original size before it is ready to bake.

Bake small loaves rather than large ones. Do not have the loaf too large for the pan; it will be a bad shape.

Biscuit and rolls require a hotter oven than bread and a longer time to rise.

A little sugar or a little Cottolene mixed with the rising will keep bread moist.

Do not put a cloth around bread or biscuit if put in a tin box.

In using baking powder or other chemicals with salt, mix them thoroughly with the flour by twice putting all through the sieve together. An even teaspoonful of baking powder to a cupful of flour is a good proportion.

Two teaspoonfuls of cream of tartar and one teaspoonful of soda is equal to two teaspoonsfuls of baking powder. *Always sift your flour.*

Bread.

(Mrs. Webb.)

Boil 3 medium sized potatoes, mash smoothly, add 1 teacupful sifted flour. Add the water in which the potatoes were boiled. When hot, beat thoroughly, then add 1 tablespoonful salt, 1 tablespoonful shortening and 1 pint cold water and ½ cake compressed yeast. Add sufficient flour to thicken, knead at once, until it will not stick to the board. Raise in covered pan over night. In the morning knead slightly and make into loaves. Raise double its size. Bake in moderate oven.

Compressed Yeast Bread.

(Juliet Corson.)

When it is possible to obtain fresh compressed yeast, also called German yeast, an excellent bread can be made in about two hours and half; the rapidity of the leavening, or "raising," the dough is advantageous, because less of the nutritive elements of the flour are lost than by following the long process; for two loaves of bread use 3 pounds of flour; about a quart of water; 2 teaspoonfuls of salt, and an ounce of fresh compressed yeast; dissolve the yeast in a pint of lukewarm water; stir into it sufficient flour to make a thick batter; cover the bowl containing the batter or sponge with a folded towel, and set it in a warm place to rise; if properly covered and heated, it will rise to a light foam in about half an hour; then stir into it the salt, dissolved in a little warm water; add the rest of the flour and sufficient lukewarm water to make a dough stiff enough to knead; knead it five minutes; divide it into two loaves, put them into buttered baking-pans, cover them with a folded towel, and set them in a warm place to rise twice their height; then bake the loaves until each one is thoroughly done. In raising the sponge, be sure that the heat is not sufficient to "scald" or harden it, as that will prevent fermentation; therefore do not place it where the hand cannot be held with comfort; keep it covered from draughts. Add the rest of the flour.

The dough made for home-made bread can be baked as raised biscuit; and it can be made a little nicer by kneading in with it a tablespoonful each of sugar and melted butter; or it can be boiled in soups and stews as raised dumplings.

To test the heat of the oven follow the method of Jules Gouffe, the celebrated *chef* of the Paris Jockey club; the "moderate oven" temperature is that degree of heat which will turn ordinary writing paper dark yellow or buff, that is, the color of kindling wood; put a sheet of paper in the oven and close the door; if the paper blazes the oven is too hot; arrange the dampers to lower the heat for ten minutes; then again test it with more paper; it may be necessary to try the temperature several times.

Premium Bread.

Take ⅓ milk and ⅔ water; thicken with flour, and for 4

medium sized loaves use 3 tablespoonfuls of yeast; set it to rise, and when light mix stiff, adding butter the size of a black walnut, and sufficient salt; mould down two or three times thoroughly before making into loaves; then mould the loaves, and as soon as light bake 1 hour in a hot oven.

Yeast for Above.

One quart water, 1 handful hops, 3 grated potatoes, medium sized, half cup sugar, half cup salt, and a teaspoonful of ground ginger. Boil the hops, strain, then add the other ingredients and boil for a couple of minutes.

Graham Bread No. 1.

One pint of water or milk, 1 yeast cake, or 1 cup of yeast. Wheat flour. About nine o'clock at night dissolve the yeast cake in the water, which should be lukewarm, and add enough wheat flour to form a stiff batter. Stir and beat the batter thoroughly for 5 minutes, leaving it full of bubbles; and set it in a warm place to rise. In the morning measure the following:

One cupful of molasses, 1 teaspoonful of soda, 2 teaspoonfuls salt. Graham flour. Dissolve the soda in a little cold water, slightly warm the molasses, and add it to the soda. Stir the salt into the sponge, and beat well with a strong spoon; then put in the molasses and soda, and when these have been thoroughly incorporated by beating, add Graham flour until a very thick mixture is formed. This is not to be kneaded like other kinds of yeast bread, but it should be so thick with Graham as to be difficult to stir. Beat the batter well for three or four minutes, turn it into two well-greased tins, and set in a warm place; and when the loaves have risen to be half again their original size, bake for an hour in a rather slow oven. The bread will not rise as rapidly as that made of wheat flour, as it has more body to carry. It is mixed so soft that the dough takes the form of the pans in which it is baked. The success of Graham bread depends largely upon thorough beating.

Rye or entire wheat may be used in place of Graham flour.

Graham Bread No. 2.

(Miss Carrie Parker.)

One pint of warm milk, 1 teaspoonful salt, 2 tablespoonfuls sugar or molasses, ½ cake of compressed yeast, ½ cup of warm water, 2½ cups of white flour, 3 cups of Graham flour. Proceed as in Graham bread No. I.

Boston Brown Bread.

(Mrs. A. G. Rogers.)

One quart of Indian meal, 1 quart rye meal, 1 cup molasses, 1 teaspoonful soda, salt to taste, 1½ quarts warm water. Bake or steam 5 hours—some people add raisins.

Plain Rolls.

One cup milk, scalded, 1 teaspoonful butter, 1 teaspoonful sugar, ½ teaspoonful salt, ¼ cake compressed yeast, ¼ cup warm water. Flour to stiffen.

Melt the butter and dissolve the sugar and salt in the hot milk. Soak the yeast in the water; when dissolved and the milk is cool, put all together, and add about one and one-quarter cups of flour, or enough to make a thick batter. Beat thoroughly, cover the bowl with plate and a cloth and place in a pan of warm water.

Let it rise about an hour, or until full of bubbles, then stir in flour enough to make a dough that can be shaped in the hand. Let it rise again, well covered, as before, and when it is light, cut it down. When it puffs up again turn it out onto the board, and knead it slightly. Pat it out a little with the rolling pin, and spread the surface with a tablespoonful of butter, softened. Fold it over toward the middle and knead it until no trace of the butter can be seen.

Divide it into portions the size of a small egg, and roll them

B. H. STINEMETZ & SON,
Hatters and Furriers,

1237 Pennsylvania Avenue.   413 Thirteenth Street.

WASHINGTON, D. C.

Specialties.
LADIES' FURS, KNOX NEW YORK HATS.
Umbrellas and Canes.

L. A. DELLWIG,
—Grocer and Provision Dealer,—

Offers real Mocha and Java Coffee of his own roasting, Black, Green and Mixed Tea, rich of flavor and strength, at fifty cents per pound. The choicest home-dressed Beef, Lamb, Veal and Pork; a full line of canned goods, and Fresh Vegetables; Fruits, pure Maple Syrup, Mincemeat, Sweet Cider and unadulterated vinegar, with a full line of Groceries as represented, or money refunded.

L. A. DELLWIG,
Cor. 2d and Mass. Ave., and D Sts., N. E.

C. S. MONTAGUE,
GROCER.

2204 14th St. Northwest.

First class goods.

Prompt service.

under the hand on the board until about a finger's length.

Place them close together in two rows in a long shallow pan. Let them rise till very light, then bake in a very quick oven.

Meat Bread.

(Mrs. Cambell.)

Two pounds beef, 1 pound ham, 2 bunches parsley, chop fine; 3 eggs, ½ cupful milk, 1 cupful cracker or bread crumbs. Pepper and salt to taste. Form into a loaf and bake in oven. Pour 1 pint of water over it after it is in pan.

Salt-Rising Bread.

(Mrs. Parker.)

One pint new milk; corn meal to thicken; 1 gallon flour; 1 tablespoonful sugar; 1 teaspoonful salt; pinch of soda.

Set the milk on the fire and stir in corn meal to make thick as mush. Set in a warm place all night. In the morning it will be light. Put the flour in a bowl, pour in the mush and mix with warm milk and water, equal parts: add the sugar, salt and soda. Make a stiff batter, cover and keep warm. In an hour it will be light. Work in flour to make stiff dough, let it rise, mold in loaves, put in greased pans, let it rise and bake. This makes the sweetest and most wholesome bread a family can use.

Brown Bread.

(H. S. B.)

One pint Indian meal, 1 pint rye, ½ pint sour milk, ½ cup molasses, 1 teaspoonful soda, and enough warm water to make thin enough to drop from a spoon.

Pumkin Bread.

(Mrs. Owens.)

Two cups buttermilk; 3 cups wheat flour; 3 cups corn meal;

1 cup stewed pumkin; 1 cup molasses; 2 heaping tablespoonfuls Cottolene; 2 eggs; ½ tablespoonful soda.

Steam 2½ hours and brown in the oven.

Sour Milk Biscuit.

(Juliet Corson.)

One quart flour; 1 tablespoonful salt; 1 teaspoonful soda; 1 pint sour milk or buttermilk.

Sift the flour with salt and baking soda; flour or butter a a pan, and see that the oven is hot; wet the flour with a pint of sour milk, or enough to make a soft dough; add 1 tablespoonful of Cottolene, by chopping it into the flour; shape the biscuits quickly, put them into the pan, and bake them in a hot oven for about twenty minutes.

Biscuit.

One quart of flour, 2 heaping teaspoonfuls of baking powder, salt, butter size of an egg, milk enough to make a soft dough; roll, and cut soft and thin.

Tea Rolls.

(Mrs. Parker.)

Two pounds flour; 6 teaspoonfuls Cottolene; 2 eggs; 2 tablespoonfuls sugar; 1 pint milk; 1 teacup yeast; little salt.

Rub the flour into the Cottolene; add salt. Beat the eggs, add the sugar, have almost boiling milk, pour it on the eggs and mix all together, then add the yeast. Let stand till light, then make in small rolls, and when light bake. These rolls are delicious and will bake in ten minutes.

Sally Lunns.

Two cups flour, 2 teaspoonfuls baking powder, ½ a teaspoonful salt, 1 egg, ½ a cup milk, ¼ cup melted butter. Bake 15 minutes in a very hot oven.

Muffins.

(Mrs. Cambell.)

One cup milk, 1 egg, small piece butter, 1 tablespoonful sugar, 2 teaspoonful yeast powder, melt butter and stir in last. Flour enough to make a stiff batter.

Graham Muffins.

(H. S. F.)

One cup graham flour, ½ cup white flour, ¼ cup sugar, 2 teaspoonful baking powder, pinch of salt, mixed well together then break 1 egg into a cup, beat well and fill with sweet milk, adding lastly butter (melted) size of a butternut mix quickly together and bake in hot pan.

Entire Wheat Gems.

Two cupfuls of entire-wheat flour, 1 cupful of cold water, ½ cupful of milk. Beat slightly and fill gempans, which should be small, deep and very hot. Bake ½ an hour in a very hot oven, the first fifteen minutes on the grate and the remainder of the time on the bottom of the oven.

Maryland or Beaten Biscuit.

One quart flour, ½ teaspoonful salt, 2 ounces of Cottolene, 1 cup cold water. Rub the Cottolene and salt into the flour and mix with cold water to a very stiff dough. Knead ten minutes, or until well mixed; then beat hard with a biscuit beater or heavy rolling pin, turning the mass over and over until it begins to blister and looks light and puffy. When in this condition pull off a small piece suddenly, form it into a round biscuit, then pinch off a bit from the top. Turn over and press with the thumbs, leaving a hollow in the centre. Put the biscuits some distance apart in the pan. Prick with a fork. Bake twenty minutes in a quick oven.

Rusk.
(Mrs. Iva Merrill.)

One pint of bread dough, 1 tumbler of warm milk, butter the size of an egg, 1 small cup of sugar, ½ teaspoonful of soda. Set to rise, when light roll out and make into rolls and let rise again until very light before putting in the oven. Bake twenty minutes.

Hot Cross Buns,

Three cups milk, 1 cup sugar, one tablespoonful butter or lard, 1 cup tepid water, 1 teaspoonful salt, ½ of a grated nutmeg, ½ a cake compressed yeast. Add sufficient flour to make a good batter; let stand in a warm place to rise. Roll out ½ an inch thick, make a deep cross on top of each bun, with a knife. Place in pans, let rise again, and bake from twenty to twenty-five minutes. Brush over the top with white of egg and 1 tablespoonful powdered sugar.

Rye Rusk.

Two teacups rye flour, ½ coffee-cup of graham flour and ½ cup wheat. Add a level teaspoonful of salt and stir together. Then add a teacup of sugar, a heaping tablespoonful of Cottolene, and a Fleischmann's compressed yeast cake dissolved in a little warm water. Mix with sufficient warm milk to make a soft batter, and put in a warm place to rise. When light add a cup of stoned raisins and a sprinkling of caraway seed if these are liked. Mix them in well, and let rise again. Bake slowly.

Corn Cake.
(Mrs. H. S. Foster.)

One half cup sour milk, ½ cup sweet milk, 1 tablespoonful cream, (either sour or sweet), 2 tablespoonfuls molasses (or sugar), 1 teaspoonful soda, 1 cup of flour, 1 cup Indian meal.

Buckwheat Cakes.

One quart of buckwheat flour, ½ teacupful of sifted corn meal, water sufficient to make soft batter, 1 tablespoonful of molasses and little salt. Mix well with warm water over night; add 1 cake of Fleischmann's compressed yeast, dissolve in warm water; set in a warm place; let rise till morning. Bake on hot griddle well greased with a piece of sweet fat salt pork. Some use oatmeal with buckwheat for cakes.

Flannel Cakes.

(Mrs. Owens.)

One pint sour milk or sour cream; 3 level teaspoonfuls melted Cottolene, if milk is used; 3 eggs; 1 teaspoonful soda; flour for batter to bake on griddle.

Leave the whites of eggs till just before baking, then beat very light and stir in lightly.

Pancakes.

(Mrs. Parker.)

One pint flour; 1 teaspoonful baking powder: 1 teaspoonful salt; 1 egg; 2 cups milk.

Make a thin batter with the above ingredients. Rub a scant teaspoonful of Cottolene over the bottom of a hot frying pan, pour in a large ladleful of batter and fry quickly. Keep warm, put in more batter. Serve with honey.

Huckleberry Griddle Cakes.

(Mrs. C. W. F.)

One-half pint huckleberries, 1½ pints flour, 1 teaspoonful salt, 1 tablespoonful brown sugar, 2 teaspoonfuls Baking Powder, 1 egg, 1 pint milk. Sift together flour, sugar, salt, and powder; add beaten egg, milk, and huckleberries (washed and picked over). Mix into batter. Have griddle hot enough to form crust soon as batter touches it. In order to confine juice of berries, turn quickly, so as to form crust on other side; turn once more on each side to complete baking. Blackberry or Raspberry Griddle Cakes in same manner.

Pop Overs.

(Hattie Barnes.)

One egg, white and yolk beaten separately, 1 cup sweet milk, 1 cup flour, a pinch of salt. Bake twenty minutes.

Snow Balls.

One cup of sugar, 1 cup of flour, 2 tablespoonfuls of sweet milk, 1 teaspoonful of Baking Powder, 3 eggs; flavor with lemon. Put 1 tablespoonful in a buttered cup, and steam twenty minutes. Roll in white sugar while hot.

Scotch Scones.

One quart flour, sifted with 2 teaspoonfuls Baking powder, 1 tablespoonful sugar, ½ teaspoonful salt, 1 tablespoonful lard, 2 beaten eggs, and a pint of sweet milk. Let rise four or five hours, and bake in muffin rings in hot oven.

Mother's Bunus.

(Mrs. C. W. F.)

A cupful each of butter and sugar, a half cupful of yeast, a cupful of scalded milk, flour to make a stiff batter, raise over night; knead well in the morning, let it rise, but not too much, knead again, throwing in a handful of cake currants, make into round cakes, set in your pans, brush over the top with a little milk and molasses, raise till pretty light and bake in a moderate oven.

Rice Cakes.

One cup of cold boiled rice, 1 pint of flour, 1 teaspoonful of salt, 2 eggs beaten light, and milk to make a tolerably thick batter. Beat all together well, and bake on griddle.

Cream Toast.

Heat 1 pint milk, stir into it one large tablespoonful flour wet with a little cold milk. Add 1 large teaspoonful butter, and 1 cup cream if you have it. Place on the back of stove to keep hot, then toast nicely some bread, dip into the cream, put into a dish, and when you have sufficient toast, pour the cream over it and serve

Fried Bread.

If the bread is very dry dip each slice quickly in water, then make a batter from 1 egg, 2 tablespoonfuls flour, and milk enough to make a thin batter; dip each slice in it and fry in butter or sweet lard, heated very hot, before laying in the bread. This makes an excellent dessert if eaten with wine or brandy sauce.

Waffles.

(Mrs. Flora M. Sprague.)

One pint sour milk; 3 tablespoonfuls melted butter; 3 eggs beaten separately; 1 teaspoonful soda, pinch of salt; flour to make stiff batter. Bake in waffle irons.

MEMORANDA.

MEMORANDA.

❋ UP TO DATE GROCERS. ❋

To Insure Success in Bread and Pastries use pure and unadulterated ingredients. You can find them in our store.

We Recommend Dakota flour. It is equal to any on the market.

Our Spices Are guarenteed to be absolutely pure by reliable importers.

Our Flavoring Extracts Are from the Leading manufactores of this country.

We Carry A full assortment of Imported and Domestic Groceries, canned goods and table delicacies.

A Trial Order Will Convince you of the purity of our goods, Your patronage is solicited. Orders by mail promptly delivered.

HART & HIGGINS,

N. W. Cor. 11th & I sts., N. W.

PIES.

*"No soil upon earth is so dear to our eyes,
As the soil we first stirred in terrestrial pies."*
O. W. HOLMES.

"Do not tell your wife that your mother's pies were better than hers."

Cottolene makes a lighter and more delicate pie-crust than lard, and there is none of the greasiness that always exists with lard while there is more of the shortening quality. Cottolene contains no salt. Always use a little in your pastry. Use ⅔ of the usual quantity of shortening when you use Cottolene. Use the Cottolene *cold*, and keep the pastry in a cold place. Having tried Cottolene, you will not want lard and very little butter for your pastry. If Cottolene or any shortening is distributed in layers throughout the pastry, without allowing a paste to be formed with the flour, it will be flaky.

The compiler heartily recommends the use of this compound after two years of practical experience as being more healthful and economical than any other shortening.

To prevent the juice of pies from soaking into the under crust, rub the crust, before filling the pies—with a cloth dipped in a well beaten egg.

Pie Crust.

(Mrs. C. W. F.)

One cupful Cottolene, 3 cupfuls of flour, a little salt. Sift the flour and the salt and rub in the shortening. Use enough ice water to hold all together, handling as little as possible, roll from you. One-third of the above quantity is enough for one pie.

For Pastry.

(Miss Nellie B. Hoyt.)

One cupful of flour is sufficient for the crust of a medium-sized pie. To make tender and flaky pastry, always mix with a knife and roll *from you*, using lard, butter and water as cold as possible. A marble or glass slab is excellent upon which to roll pastry.

Common Pie Crust.

(Mrs. S.)

One cupful of lard, 1 cupful of butter, 5 cupsful of flour, ½ a teaspoonful of baking powder, cut the lard and butter into the flour with a knife; add just enough ice water to mix. Neither roll nor knead more than necessary.

As Easy Way of Making Light Pastry.

(Sadie B.)

Chop ¾ of a cupful of butter into a cupful of sifted flour, with a pinch of salt. Mix with a few spoonfuls of ice water into a stiff paste. Roll out once or twice with a little more flour.

Apple Pie.

Six tart apples, ½ cupful sugar, ½ lemon rind grated. Peel, core, and slice apples very thin; line pie plate with paste; put in apples, sugar, and a little water; spice to taste, wet the edges with cold water; wash with milk, bake in steady moderate oven 25 minutes—or till apples are cooked.

Blackberry or Huckleberry Pie.

One-half cupful sugar, and 3 cupfuls berries to each pie. Line pie plate with paste, put in berries and sugar, wet the edge, cover and wash with milk; bake in quick, steady oven 20 minutes

Custard Pie.

Four eggs, 1 quart of milk, a little salt, and ½ cupful of sugar. Bake with under crust only.

Cocoanut Pie.

One grated cocoanut, 1 quart of milk heated to boiling and poured over the grated nut, 2 tablespoonfuls of butter, 4 eggs, sugar to taste. This makes two pies.

Whipped Cream Pie.

("Grand-ma.")

Line a deep pie tin with a moderately rich crust. Bake in a quick oven; then spread it with any soft jam or jelly, and on this pour a teacupful of cream, beaten or whipped to a stiff foam; then sweeten and flavor to taste; the cream will beat more easily if very cold at first. More jelly can be spread on the top of the cream, or serve it without, as preferred.

Rhubard Pie.

(L. S. P.)

Cut up fine 2 cupfuls of tender rhubard, add ⅔ cupful of sugar and a rounded spoonful of flour; stir all together and lay on an under crust, put a few pieces of butter on the top, grate over a little nutmeg, cover and bake half an hour, or till just cooked through. Prepared in this way the juice will not run out.

Pineapple Pie.

One large pineapple or 2 small ones (chop quite fine), 2 cups sugar, 3 tablespoonsfuls cornstarch, 3 eggs, 1 cup sweet milk or water, a little salt. This fills three pies. Bake with two crusts.

Genuine Pumkin Pies.

(Mrs. C. W. F.)

These shall really be pumkin, and neither squash nor custard. The pumkin should be of dark yellow skin and heavy in proportion to its size; the flesh thick and fine grained; pare and cut in inch cubes and cook it in a little water until soft, being careful that it does not burn. Then press through a colander, put it back in the kettle with some molasses or sugar and spice, and let it mull away until it is a rich red amber marmalade. This must be done a day or two before the pies are made, for it is a work of time. One cupful of such pumkin is ample for a deep pie, and real pumkin pie is never baked in a shallow plate. A proportion for a pie is 1 cupful of pumkin, 1 egg, 3 to 4 cups of milk, ½ cupful of sugar, a little salt, ½ teaspoonful of ginger, ¼ teaspoonful of cinnamon and a little nutmeg. Bake rather slowly.

Summer Mince Pie.

(H. S. B.)

One cup rasins chopped fine, 3 cups water, 3 cups sugar, ½ cup vinegar, 1 nutmeg, 1 tablespoonful each of cinnamon, cloves, allspice and ginger, butter size of an egg, 8 crackers rolled fine. Cook well before baking. This quantity makes four or five pies.

Mince Meat.

If the perfection of flavor is to be obtained, mince-meat should be made two, or better, three weeks before it will be needed. If made according to the following recipe, it will keep all Winter, and the quantity given will make a great many pies:

Two pounds of beef, 2 pounds of suet, ¼ pound of candied lemon peel, 2 pounds of layer raisins, 1 quart of sherry, 1 quart of good brandy, 2 oranges (juice and rind), 2 lemons (juice and rind), 2 tablespoonfulfs of salt, 4 pounds of apples, 2 pounds of currants, 2 pounds of sultana raisins, 1 pound of citron, 2 pounds of sugar, 2 nutmegs (grated), ¼ ounce of mace, ½ ounce of cinnamon, ¼ ounce of cloves.

Cover the beef with boiling water, cook it gently until tender, and set it away to cool. When it is cool, chop it fine, and also the suet and apples; stone the layer raisins and shave the citron. Mix all the dry ingredients well together, and add the juice and grated rinds of the lemons and oranges. Mix well, pack away in a stone jar, add the wine and brandy, and set in a cool place, closely covered. When ready to use, thin the required quantity with cider.

Pasadina Orange Pie.

(K. D. Barnes.)

Grated rind of 1 large orange and juice of 2, 1 cup sugar, yolks of 3 eggs. Reserve the whites for the meringue. A tablespoonful of flour, a little salt. A little lemon juice adds to the flavor.

Filling for Lemon Pie.

(Edith M. Ryder.)

Four large crackers rolled fine, juice and rind of 1 lemon, ⅔ of a cupful of sugar, ¾ of a cupful of water, yolks of 2 eggs and a lump of butter. Bake with one crust. Beat whites of the eggs and spread over the pie when baked.

Apple Roll.

(Mrs. Nellie B. Hoyt.)

Make a dough a little richer than for biscuit. Roll about half inch thick. Chop your apples fine and spread the dough thick with them. Then sprinkle with sugar and cinnamon. Turn the sides toward the center and proceed to roll it up. Bake half an hour. To be eaten with cream or a rich wine sauce.

Old Fashioned Lemon Pie.

(Mrs. C. W. F.)

The juice and grated rind of 2 lemons, 2 rolled crackers, 1 egg,

1 cupful sugar, ⅔ cupful water, 1 cupful chopped raisins, 1 tablespoonful butter, salt and spices to taste. Bake with two crusts.

Pan Dowdy.

Line a deep dish with paste made of sweet cream, flour, little salt and baking powder. Fill the dish with sour apples cut in slices, sweeten with ½ cup brown sugar and ½ cup molasses, add salt and spices to taste, place across the top of the apple, thinly cut stripes of fat salt pork. Cover with crust and bake half an hour. Serve hot with sauce.

MEMORANDA.

—SUCCESSOR TO—

JOSEPH F. PAGE,

Grocer and Dealer in Fine Teas.

1210 F STREET, NORTHWEST

Manufacturer's Agent for the Celebrated

FLORENCE OIL STOVES,

Shaw's Cone Gas Stoves, Florence Light, and Pratt's Astral Oils.

AGENTS WANTED.

Telephone or postal orders promptly executed.

NO LIQUORS SOLD.

Just received large consignment of Nuts, Raisins and Fruits suitable for Holiday trade.

PUDDINGS and SAUCES.

*"Your dressing, dancing, gadding, where is the good in?
Sweet lady, tell me, can you make a pudding?"*

Puddings are either baked, boiled or steamed; rice, bread, custard and fruit puddings require moderate heat; batter and corn starch, a quick oven. Always bake them as soon as mixed. In making puddings, always beat the eggs separately, straining the yolks and adding the white the last thing. When fruit is used, roll it in flour and stir it in toward the last. Boiled puddings are lighter when boiled in a cloth, bring the cloth or pudding-bag out of hot water, flour the inside, pour in the pudding, tie securely and place in a kettle with a saucer in the bottom to prevent burning and pour in boiling water to cover the bag. Keep it boiling constantly, turning several times. It requires double the time to boil that it does to bake a pudding. Boiled puddings should be served as soon as done. Steaming is a safter method of cooking, as the pudding is sure to be light and wholesome. In making sauces, do not boil after the butter is added.

Apple Dumplings.

(Mrs. Keech.)

Rub equal quantities of butter and lard and a little salt into flour, with yeast powder, as for biscuit, and stir through this the apples chopped fine. Make into balls and drop into boiling water.

Plum Pudding.

(Mrs. Chas. Merrill.)

Three fourths pound of suet, chopped fine, 1 pound of sugar, 1 pound of grated stale bread, 1 pound of stoned raisins, 1 pound of currants, ½ pint of milk and a gill of brandy, 1 nutmeg, ½ teaspoon of cinnamon, ½ teaspoon mace, the rind and juice of a lemon, 1 teaspoon salt and nine eggs. Mix all the ingredients except the eggs, which should be beaten until light and then added. Steam 5 hours.

Mother's Suet Pudding.

(Mrs. C. W. F.)

One cup chopped suit, 1 cup stoned raisins, ½ cup currents, 1 cup molasses, 1 cup sour milk, 1 egg, 3 cups flour, salt and ½ teaspoonful soda. All kinds of spices. Steam 3 hours.

Blueberry Pudding.

(Mrs. Wm. Merrill.)

One cup sweet milk, 1 cup of molasses or sugar, flour enough to make a stiff batter for a spoon to stand in, 1 teaspoonful soda, just before putting in a quart of berries. Steam 3 hours. The success of the pudding is said to be in adding the soda the last thing. ½ makes a large pudding. Eat with liquid or hard sauce.

Snow Pudding.

(Miss Helen L. Johnson,)

Editor, *Table Talk*.

Soak ½ a box of gelatine in ½ cup of cold water for ½ an hour; pour over it 1 pint of boiling water and then dissolve; add ¾ of a pound of granulated sugar, and ½ of a cup of lemon juice; stir until the sugar is dissolved, strain into a basin. Stand when it is cold, not only until the liquid has cooled, but has begun to foam. It must be beaten until it is as white as snow before the eggs are added. Beat the white of three eggs to a stiff white froth. Beat them into the mixture, and when thoroughly mixed snowy white and stiff, turn into a mold previously wet with cold water. The liquid settles because it is not beaten sufficiently, or is beaten before it begins to foam. It must be beaten stiff and foam before the eggs are added. Then there is no danger of their rising.

Banana Pudding.

(Miss Helen Johnson.)

(Editor *Table Talk*.)

Cut stale cake in thin slices and line a dish with the pieces. Cover the cake with bananas sliced very thin. Pour over this a cupful of rather thin boiled custard. Make another layer of the cake and bananas, and cover with the custard. Set away in the cold until time to serve.

Rice Pudding.

("Home Gleanings.")

One-third cup rice, 1 quart milk, 1 tablespoon of butter, ½ cup sugar, salt and vanilla. Bake slowly for 4 hours, stirring occasionally the first hour.

Steamed Indian Pudding.

(Mrs. L. P. Hosford.)

One pint sour milk, 2 eggs, 1½ cups Indian meal, 2 small tablespoons beef suet, 2 tablespoons molasses, ½ teaspoonful each of cinnamon and ground ginger. Little salt, pinch of soda. Heat the milk boiling hot, add the soda and pour upon the meal. Stir well, add the suet powdered and the salt. When this mixture is cold put with it the eggs beaten light, the molasses and the spices, and beat all hard. Turn into a well greased mold and steam for three hours. Eat with hard sauce. This quantity will serve eight or ten persons.

Indian Pudding.

(Mrs. Buhsen.)

One quart milk ; when boiling add 7 tablespoons Indian meal, 1 cup cold water. Then add 1 egg, 1 tablespoon of ginger, two-thirds of a cup of molasses and a little salt. Bake one hour. Sweet apples or raisins may be added.

Chocolate Pudding.

(Harriman Cook Book.)

One-half cup of hot water poured on 1 square of chocolate, stir and let come to a boil, and then add ½ cup of milk, ½ cup sugar, 1 tablespoonful of cornstarch. Boil until thick, then add 1 pinch of salt and flavor with vanilla.

Custard for Pudding.

Boil 1 cup of milk, add 1 egg, ½ cup of sugar, 1 teaspoonful of corn starch, ½ teaspoonful of flour. Boil and add a pinch of salt and flavor with lemon.

Gem Peach Pudding.

(Mrs. Bates.)

Sift well together 2 cups flour, ½ teaspoonful salt and 1 heaping teaspoonful yeast powder. Chop in 2 ounces butter ; beat 2 eggs light and add to ½ cup water ; beat briskly and stir quickly into the flour, making a very stiff batter ; beat vigorously ; then drop a spoonful of batter into each well buttered gem pan, place on top, half a peach either fresh or canned ; cover with another spoonful batter and bake in a quick oven for 30 minutes. Serve hot with sweetened cream. This quantity will make 8 little puddings.

Prune Pudding.

(Miss Helen Johnson.)

(Editor *Table Talk*.)

Wash half a pound of prunes, cover with cold water and let

stand over night. In the morning cook until tender, then press through a colander; add three-quarters of a cup of granulated sugar, stir until it is dissolved. Beat the whites of four eggs to a stiff, dry froth, add them carefully to the prunes and bake twenty minutes in a quick oven. Serve at once with cream.

Cocoanut Pudding.

(Mrs. C. W. F.)

Three slices of bread soaked in 1 pint of milk. Take 3 eggs—separate yolks from white. Beat the yolks well into the bread, using 1 egg at a time, adding 1 ounce of butter. Take half a pound of desiccated cocoanut, and mix with the bread, adding another pint of milk, sweetening to taste. Beat the whites of the eggs to a froth, and mix with the compound just before baking. Put in a moderately hot oven, and bake for one hour.

Cherry Roly Poly.

(Miss Worick.)

Make a light paste as for apple dumplings; roll in oblong sheet and fill with cherries—sour if possible. Sprinkle with sugar, roll closely, folding the end over carefully to preserve the syrup. Boil in a pudding bag one and one-half hours, and serve with hot sweet sauce.

Nesselrode Pudding.

(Miss Helen L. Johnson.)

(Editor *Table Talk*.)

[Copyrighted.]

One pint chestnuts, yolks 4 eggs, 1 pint cream, 1 tablespoonful vanilla, 1 cup syrup from preserved pineapple, 1 cup water, 2 ounces citron, 2 ounces candied cherries, 2 ounces pineapple, 2 ounces sultana raisins, 1 pound sugar.

Shell the chestnuts, remove the thin brown skins, and put

them in a saucepan with sufficient boiling water to cover. Simmer twenty minutes or until soft. Mash and press them through a colander. Cut the fruit in small pieces, put the sugar and water in a saucepan over the fire, stir until the syrup spins a thread, add to it the cup of pineapple syrup and pour over the fruit. Scald 1 cup of cream. Heat the yolks of the eggs very light, and add to the scalded cream on the fire and stir for 2 minutes. Add the chestnut pulp; mix well, take from the fire, and press through a sieve. When cold flavor with vanilla and sherry and freeze. When nearly frozen, beat in the fruit and the remaining cup of cream beaten stiff and dry. Mix well with a spoon. Cover and finish freezing. Remove the dasher and pack.

Orange Pudding.

(Harrison Cook-Book.)

Four oranges, slice thin, lay in deep dish. Pour 1 cup sugar over them and let stand 1 hour. Cream; ½ cup flour, ¾ cup sugar, yolks 3 eggs, small piece butter, vanilla. Beat all together, add 1 pint boiling milk. Heat a few minutes and pour over oranges. Frosting.—Beat the whites of 3 eggs and 2 tablespoonfuls sugar. Put this on the cream and brown in the oven. Pudding to be eaten cold.

Lemon Snow Pudding.

(Mrs. Jay F. Bancroft.)

Take the juice of 1 lemon, 1 cup sugar, 2 tablespoonfuls corn starch, stir into them 1 pint boiling water; cook a few minutes, then pour it over the whites of three eggs. Stir all together, place in cups on the ice. Make a custard of 1 pint milk, the yolks of 3 eggs, 2 tablespoonfuls sugar, flavor with vanilla. When ready to serve turn the snow onto plates with the custard around it.

SAUCES.

Hard Sauce.

(Miss Helen L. Johnson.)

(Editor *Table Talk*.)

[Copyrighted.]

Beat ¼ of butter to a cream, add gradually ½ of a cup of powdered sugar, stirring constantly and beat until very light. Add the unbeaten whites of 2 eggs, 1 at a time, throughly amalgamating one before adding the next. Add 1 teaspoonful of vanilla, stir until well mixed; then add liquor if used, 1 tablespoonful of sherry or brandy. Mix well, mold, and put in the ice box to harden before using.

Spanish Sauce.

One-half cup of boiling water, 1 tablespoonful of corn starch, 2 tablespoonfuls of vinegar, 1 tablespoonful of cottolene, 1 cup sugar or molasses, ½ nutmeg.

Cold Cream Sauce.

Beat together a cup of sugar and ½ a cup of butter; add a cup of cream. Stir all to a thick, even liquid, flavor with lemon or vanilla, and place on ice until ready to serve.

Everyday Sauce.

A pint of boiling water, a heaping teacup of sugar, a tablespoonful of butter, pinch of salt, and a tablespoonful of corn starch dissolved in cold water. Boil ½ an hour. Season with nutmeg or flavor with a tablespoonful of current jelly liquefied in a tablespoonful of hot water.

Foaming Sauce.

Melt a teacupful of sugar in a little water; let it boil; stir in a glass of wine and whisk in the well-beaten whites of three eggs. Serve at once.

MEMORANDA.

MEMORANDA.

STANDARD SEWING MACHINE
ROOMS.
JOSEPH H. FISKE, Manager.

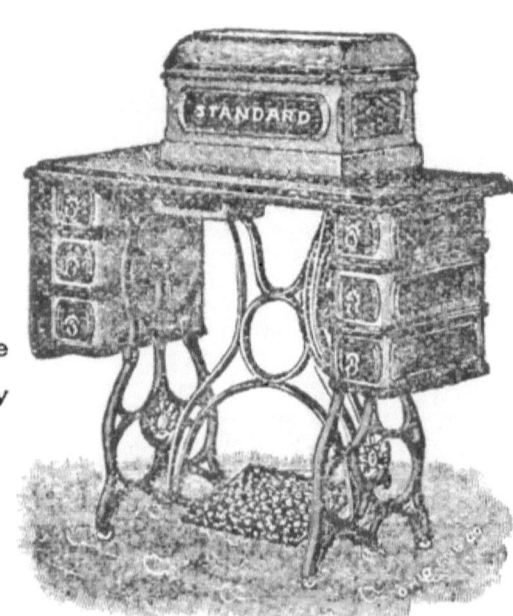

Try the Standard before buying any other.

The Celebrated Imperial Pinned Paper Patterns.

602 9TH STREET,
UNDER
Masonic Temple.

DESSERTS AND FANCY DISHES.

"To be good, be useful. To be useful, be always making something good."

Desserts were never more delicious, more easily prepared, or more to the taste of the epicure than they are to-day.

To many people, the dessert of desserts is figs; one fig and a slice of caramel or pound cake; the second choice is a brandy-fig with cream sponge cake; cherries with walnut cake is another delicate finish for a nice dinner, and brandy cherries with angel cake will be found equally choice.

A saucerful of whipped cream made very sweet and decorated with an edging of big, ripe strawberries is good to eat and pretty to look at. The same cream moulded in a wine glass, turned out on a plate and encircled with tart cranberry jelly is a dainty dessert.

Shaddock Sherbert.

(Miss Helen L. Johnson.)

(Editor *Table Talk*.)

[Copyrighted.]

Cut 6 shaddocks into halves. Remove the seeds, and with an

orange spoon, take out the pulp. Put 2½ cups of sugar over the fire with 1 cup of water; stir until the sugar is dissolved; boil until the sirup spins a thread. Cover 2 tablespoonfuls of gelatine with ¼ a cup of cold water and let stand for ½ hour. Dissolve over hot water. Add the hot sirup to the shaddock pulp with the gelatine. Let cool, press through a sieve and freeze.

Orange Sherbert.

(Mrs. M. C. Currier.)

Six juicy oranges. After pressing out the juice put water on pulp to get out remaining juice, if oranges are sweet add juice of 2 or 3 lemons, sweeten, and just before freezing, add 1 pint of good cream. Add water sufficient to make ½ gallon.

Tutti Frutti.

(Harriman Cook-Book.)

Sweeten and flavor 1 gallon rich cream; when partly frozen, stir in 1 can pineapple, citron, raisins, figs, candies and freeze.

Spanish Cream.

(Mrs. James Campbell.)

One pint milk, ½ package of gelatine soaked ½ an hour in the milk, then put in a kettle and stir till all is dissolved and the milk reaches the boiling point. Beat the yolks of 3 eggs with 1 cup of sugar, and stir into the hot milk. Then remove from the fire and stir in the beaten whites of the eggs, flavor with vanilla. Beat well, then pour into a dish and set on the ice.

Apple Float.

(Mrs. Wm. Merrill.)

One pint sifted apple sauce, 1 quart rich milk or cream. Sweeten and flavor to taste. Add the whites of 2 eggs and freeze.

Peach Glace Meringue.

(Miss Helen L. Johnson.)

Editor *Table Talk.*)

[Copyrighted.]

Scald 1 cup of cream, add 1½ cups of sugar. Stir until the sugar is dissolved and cook until the cream looks blue—about five minutes. Take from the fire, add 1 cup of uncooked cream, and, when cold, 1 teaspoonful of vanilla, and freeze. Peel 1 quart of peaches, cut in pieces and press through sieve. When the cream is frozen, add the peaches; turn the dasher rapidly until they are well stirred in. Remove the dasher. Stir down the ice cream; cover and pack. Let stand two hours to ripen before filling meringue shells.

Tapioca Cream.

(Mrs. L. P. Hosford.)

Two tablespoonfuls tapioca soaked over night. Heat 1 pint of milk to boiling. Stir in the tapioca and let it cook a few minutes. Add the yolks of 2 eggs, salt, ½ cup sugar, cook a little and when taken off the range stir in the whites beaten to a stiff froth. Flavor to taste.

Shredded Pineapples.

(Miss Elizabeth C. Hills.)

Select a ripe, juicy pineapple, remove every bit of the skin and all the "eyes." Then lay the fruit on a platter, hold it firmly with the left hand, and with a silver fork tear off the pineapple in small pieces, leaving the core whole. Put the shredded fruit in a serving dish, sprinkle generously with fine granulated sugar, cover, and let stand in the ice chest an hour, if possible, before serving. This method of preparing it draws out the juice and flavor better than slicing, and makes the fruit seem much more tender.

Charlotte Russe.
(Miss Hattie Barnes.)

Soak ¼ box gelatine in ¼ cup cold water. Line a pint mold with lady fingers. Chill and whip 1 pint cream. Set bowl in ice water. Sift over the whipped cream ⅓ cup powdered sugar, add 1 teaspoonful vanilla. Dissolve gelatine in ¼ cup boiling water. Strain it into the cream and beat rapidly. When nearly stiff pour into mold and set away to cool.

Ice Cream.
(Mrs. C. W. F.)

For 4 quarts cream when frozen, 2 quarts milk, 1 quart cream, 1 pound pulverized sugar, ½ box gelatine. Dissolve the gelatine into the warm milk, add sugar, lastly the cream, flavor to taste; if vanilla is used, 3 teaspoonfuls are sufficient. Do not cook it, but freeze at once. Freeze sufficiently hard to be easily dipped with a spoon from the freezer to the packing can, for if it is frozen too hard, the cream becomes as butter. The ice and salt in the packing tub, around the can will complete the work. Fruit of any kind may be added.

Pistachio Ice Cream.
(Mrs. E. J. Shephard.)

Blanch 3 ounces of pistachio nuts and chop them very fine. If they seem dry cover with 1 tablespoonful of sherry or a few drops of rose water and let stand for some time. Scald 1 pint of cream, add 1 cup of sugar, stir until it is dissolved and cook until the cream looks blue and thin. Take from the fire, add 1 pint of raw cream and cool. When cold, add the nuts and flavor with 1 teaspoonful of vanilla, 1 teaspoonful of pistachio, extract and color a delicate green. Turn into the freezer and freeze.

Orange Water Ice.
(Mrs. John Patterson.)

One quart water, 1 pound sugar, juice of 4 oranges, 1 teaspoonful Baker's extract of lemon, 2 teaspoonful Baker's extract of orange. Dissolve the sugar in the water, add the orange juice and flavoring extracts, and freeze.

Cherry Water Ice.

(Mrs. Stephen Rider.)

Stone 1 pound of cherries; put 1 pound of sugar, with 1 pint of water, in a saucepan over the fire; stir until the sugar is dissolved and boil for 10 minutes. Pour it over the cherries and let stand until cooled, then squeeze through a bag. When all the juice is extracted, color a delicate lavender and flavor with two drops of nectarine extract, and freeze.

Sliced Oranges.

(Mrs. C. W. F.)

Oranges sliced with grated cocoanut, are very fine to eat with cake. Slice the oranges, sprinkle with sugar, let stand a few hours. Cover with cocoanut.

Bananas and Whipped Cream.

(Mrs. C. W. F.)

Cut the bananas into small slices, and over this pour cream beaten to a stiff froth. Do not sweeten the cream until after it is whipped, and then use powdered sugar. Flavor with sherry or brandy.

P. G. McCOMAS,
Pharmacist,
1801 VERMONT AVE., N. W.
WASHINGTON, D. C.

———Manufacturer of———

EMULSOLATUM.
—FOR—
Coughs, Colds and Consumption.

WHY NOT BUY A GAS STOVE OF C. A. MUDDIMAN?
ALL STYLES 30 cents to $30.
BAKE, BOIL AND BROIL ON GAS STOVE.

614 TWELFTH STREET.

W. L. MATHEWS,
DEALER IN
Groceries, Meats and Provisions,
S. W. COR. 10TH AND S STREETS, N. W.

CAKES.

*" With weights and measures just and true,
  Oven of even heat,
Well buttered tins and quiet nerves
  Success will be complete."*

Successful cake-making depends on proper materials ; a correct recipe ; following directions explicitly; accurate weights and measurements ; compounding the ingredients in their proper order ; regulating the temperature of the oven according to the kind of cake made ; sifting the baking powder and flour together two or three times ; placing in the oven as soon as the baking powder is added ; greasing the tin with Cottolene rather than butter, and sifting a little dry flour over ; opening and shutting the oven door very gently during the process of baking ; not turning while in the oven if it can be avoided ; keeping fruit over night in a warm room, dredging it thoroughly with flour, and stirring it in lightly the last thing ; lining tins for loaf-cake with oiled paper.

To cream the butter, if it be hard, pour boiling water into the bowl, let it stand a minute, empty, wipe the bowl dry, and put in the butter ; work with a heavy spoon until soft, then beat it to a cream ; add the sugar next and beat until white and creamy ; add the well beaten yolks of the eggs, and the milk or water next, a little at a time, beating well, add part of the flour and beat from three to five minutes ; last add the flour that contains the baking powder and the whites at the same time. Whip them lightly and quickly in; do not beat a moment after they are whipped in. Never stir a cake; hold the bowl in a slanting position, and whip with a circular motion upward, carrying the spoon out of the batter each time; this incorporates more air than by the stirring method, and yields a fine-grained, light, and tender cake even with much less butter than when carelessly made. In using Cottolene which is the best shortening, put a pinch of salt in the flour.

Always flavor a cake.

Sweet milk makes a cake which cuts like pound cake. Sour milk makes spongy light cake. Do not use both in the same cake.

For rich cakes use powdered sugar. For plain cakes granlated sugar. For fine cakes, beat the yolks and whites of eggs separately. For plain cakes, beat both together thoroughly. Use of Cottelene two-thirds of the usual quantity of shortening.

In baking loaf cake remember that unless you place a piece of paper over for protection at first, a top crust will be formed at once that prevents the raising. When cake is well raised remove paper for browning on top.

Set a dish of water in the oven with cake when baking and it will seldom scorch.

Two apples kept in the cake box will keep moderately rich cake moist for a length of time, if the apples are renewed when withered.

Angel Cake.

Whites of 11 eggs, ½ cup granulated sugar sifted once, 1 cup flour sifted with 1 teaspoonful cream of tartar 4 times, 1 teaspoonful vanilla. Bake in an ungreased pan 40 minutes. When done invert pan on two cups and let stand until cake is cold.

Every Day Cake.

(Mrs. Peetrey.)

Two eggs, well beaten, 1 cup of sugar, ½ cup of butter and lard mixed, ⅔ cup of milk, 2¼ cups of flour, one teaspoonful of baking powder. Bake in 3 layers. Use any desired filling.

Feather Cake.

(Mrs. Flora Sprague.)

One cup white sugar; 1 tablespoonful butter; 1 egg; 2 even cups flour; ⅔ cup of milk; 1½ teaspoonfuls baking powder; flavor.

Corn Starch Cake.

(Mrs. J. F. Bancroft.)

Two cups sugar, ⅔ cup butter, 4 egg whites, 1 cup sweet milk, 1 cup corn starch, 2 cups flour, 2 teaspoonfuls baking powder, 2 teaspoonfuls extract of lemon. Mix in the order named. Bake ¾ of an hour, or until done, with a steady fire.

Sponge Cake.

Two eggs, 1 cup sugar, 1 cup sifted flour, 2 teaspoonfuls baking powder, ½ cup boiling water just before putting in the oven. Bake 20 minutes. The above can be baked in layers if desired.

Caramel Cake.

Three-fourths cup butter, 1½ cups sugar, 3 eggs, ¼ cup water, 1¾ cups flour, 3 ounces melted chocolate, 3 teaspoonfuls yeast powder. For filling, 2 cups of granulated sugar, whites of 2 eggs, gill boiling water, 1 teaspoonful vanilla. Pour boiling water on sugar and boil until it will candy in water, then pour syrup on 2 eggs well beaten and add vanilla.

Roll Jelly Cake.

(Mrs. W. L. Hart.)

Three eggs beaten separately, 1 cup sugar, 2 tablespoonfuls sweet milk, 1 heaping teaspoonful of baking powder, 1 cup sugar, flavor and bake in moderately hot oven, remove from pan, and lay on a cloth wet with cold water. Spread with jelly and roll quickly, sprinkle with powdered sugar.

Ice Water Sponge Cake.

(Mrs. Chas. Merrill.)

One and a half cups of sugar, 1½ cups of flour, 3 eggs, ½ cup ice-water, and 1½ teaspoonfuls of baking powder. Beat yolks and sugar with 1 tablespoonful of water, thoroughly. Better than any tea-egg cake ever eaten.

English Walnut Cake.

(Miss Helen S. Foster.)

One-half cup butter, 1½ cups sugar, ¾ cup sweet milk, 2 cups flour, 2 teaspoonfuls baking powder, whites 4 eggs, 1 cup of nuts chopped. Frost and cut in square pieces, placing one half of a nut upon each square.

Pasadena Orange Cake.

(Mrs. K. D. Barnes.)

One cup sugar, butter about size of an egg, 2 eggs beaten separately, ⅔ cup milk, 2 cups flour, 2 teaspoonfuls baking powder. Flavor. Bake in layers. Icing.—Take white of 1 egg, grated rind and juice of 1 orange. Add enough sugar to make a smooth icing and one that will spread easily without running off. Spread between layers and on top.

Marble Cake.

(Mrs. Wilcox.)

One cup of butter, 2 cups of sugar, 4 eggs, 1 cup of sweet milk, 3 cups of flour, 2 teaspoonfuls of baking powder, flavor to suit. When mixed take a teaspoonful of batter and stir in a large spoonful of chocolate and a little milk, fill your pan with about an inch of the cake and drop in 2 or 3 places a spoonful of the dark material and then another layer of cake and so on.

White Cake.

(Mrs. A. Fisher.)

Two cups pulverized sugar, 1 cup of butter, 3 cups of flour with 2 heaping teaspoonfuls of baking powder, the whites of 10 eggs, 2 teaspoonfuls of corn starch dissolved in ½ cup of sweet milk. Bake in moderate oven.

Ribbon Cake.

(Miss S. Maria Davis.)

Two cups sugar, 1 cup butter, 1 cup milk, 3 eggs, 3 cups flour, 2 teaspoonfuls baking powder. Use enough of the above for 2 layers. Into the remaining, put 1 cup of chopped raisins, ⅓ cup citron, 2 tablespoonfuls of molasses, spices of all kinds, ½ teaspoonful of each. Add a little more flour and bake as one layer. Put layers together with jelly or cooked frosting.

Lemon Layer Cake.

(Miss Helen S. Foster.)

One half cup butter, ½ cup milk, ½ cup sugar, 2 cups flour, 3 eggs beaten separately, 2 teaspoonfuls baking powder. Filling, 1 lemon, 1 cup sugar, 1 cup boiled water, 1 cup eggs, 1 tablespoonful corn starch, piece butter size of a walnut. Cook in double boiler.

Wedding Cake.

(Mrs. Flora Sprague.)

Two pounds sugar, 2 pounds butter, 2 pounds flour, 6 pounds raisins, 2 pounds figs (chopped), 2 pounds currants, 2 pounds almonds, 1½ pounds citron, 20 eggs, 1 pint brandy, 1 pint wine, 1 ounce nutmeg, 1 ounce mace, 1 ounce cinnamon, 1 ounce cloves. This will keep for years.

Molasses Layer Cake.

(Mrs. Wilcox.)

One cup of sugar, ½ cup of molasses, ½ cup butter, ½ cup buttermilk, 3 cups flour, 2 eggs, whites and yolks beaten separately, 1 teaspoonful of soda, 1 of cinnamon, ½ of cloves pulverized sugar and lemon juice between the layers.

Ginger Bread,

(Mrs. C. W. F.)

One cup molasses, ½ cup sugar, 1 cup boiling water, ⅓ cup cottolene, 1 teaspoonful soda, 1 teaspoonful ginger, pinch of salt, flour to make very stiff batter.

Pound Cake.

(Mrs. H. D. Bates.)

Beat 6 eggs to a froth, add 1 pound sugar, ½ pound butter. Beat well together. Add 1 pound flour, well mixed with 2 scant teaspoonfuls baking powder; flavor to taste. Bake in quick oven.

Fruit Cake.

(Mrs. J. W. Webb.)

One pound flour, 1 pound sugar, 1 cup molasses, 1¼ pound butter, 10 eggs, 8 pounds raisins, 4 pounds currants, 2 pounds citron, 2 pounds figs, ½ pound orange peel, ½ pound blanched almonds, 1 wine glass rose water, 1 wine glass sherry, 1 wine glass brandy. Mix butter and sugar together thoroughly, after which add eggs, then flour and fruit, which must be chopped fine.

White Fruit Cake.

(Mrs. Sprague.)

Sift 1 pound of flour with 2 teaspoonfuls of baking powder. Cream 1 pound of sugar and ½ a pound of butter together, mix with the flour, beat well and add 1 teacup of sliced citron, 1 cup of blanched almonds, 1 teacup of stoned raisins and 3 of grated cocoanut, lastly stir in carefully the well-beaten whites of 14 eggs, thin with ½ a cup of sweet milk, and pour in a greased mold. Bake two hours.

Plain Raisin Cake.

(Mrs. H. D. Bates.)

One cup sour milk, 1 cup sugar, ½ cup butter, 2 cups flour, 1 egg, 1 teaspoonful soda, 1 cup chopped raisins, spice to taste.

To Make Icing Stick.

Sift flour over the cake and then wipe off with a napkin.

[Miss Helen L. Johnson says in *Table Talk*.]

The various icings used by the pastry cook and confectioner are compounded in a different way from the numerous home icings, the latter, being as a general rule, preferable. Confectioners usually put on several coatings of icings, allowing each to dry before adding the next. The first is what is called the rough coat and is used to set the crumbs so that they may not show through the surface of the finished cake.

Transparent Icing.

(Miss Helen L. Johnson.)

Dissolve 1½ cups of granulated sugar in ½ cup of water. Let it boil without stirring until it forms a ball when picked up in the forefinger. Take from the fire and beat until it becomes a little cloudy. Put in the farina boiler and melt; let cool until, when poured on the cake, it will form, or if the cakes are small they can be dipped in it.

Confectioner's Icing.

The whites of 2 eggs, the same quantity of water; stir very thick with confectioner's sugar and flavor to suit fancy. Many use water without the eggs, but the sugar must be the special kind called XXX.

For pink icing, add a few drops of cochineal or beet juice to any white icing. Yellow may be made by using a spoonful of saffron water or two or three drops of butter color, or, better still, simply beat the yolks quite stiff with the sugar. If green is desired, use a little spinach juice. Brown is made with cocoa or chocolate.

Delicate Icing.

One cup of sugar, 3 spoonfuls of water; boil until it ropes, then pour slowly over the stiffly beaten whites of 2 eggs, stirring all the time. Flavor with almond or rose, spread while warm. Add cocoanut if desired.

Fig Filling for Cake.

(S. M. D.)

One half pound figs boiled in water to keep from burning, when soft chop with ⅔ cup of raisins (seeded). Add 1 cup sugar, juice of 1 lemon.

Chocolate Frosting.

(H. S. B.)

One cup sugar, 2 squares chocolate, 6 tablespoonfuls milk. Boil until cooked sufficiently to harden, then put on the cake—flavor with vanilla.

Caramel Frosting.

(H. S. B.)

Two-thirds cup milk, butter size of walnut, 2 cups sugar. Boil 10 minutes, flavor with vanilla, beat till cold.

Icing That Will not Crack.

Icing for cakes may be prevented from cracking when being cut by adding 1 teaspoonful of sweet cream to each unbeaten egg; beat all together and add sugar until as stiff as can be stirred.

A Delicious Shortcake.

(Mrs. C. W. F.)

Mix 1 pint of flour, 1 large teaspoonful of baking powder, and ⅓ cup of shortening. Moisten with milk. While this is baking, slice bananas in proportion of 3 to 1 orange, grate a little lemon peel and mix with 1 cup of sugar. When the cake is baked, split it and fill with the fruit. Beat enough cream stiff to pile over the top of the cake.

Apricot Shortcake.

(Mrs. Currier.)

Three cups flour, 2 teaspoonfuls baking powder, ½ teaspoonful salt, ⅓ cup butter. Rub the butter into the flour, beat 1 egg thoroughly, add 1 cup milk and stir into flour. Put dough into 2 shallow pans, sprinkle tablespoonful of sugar over each layer, bake in hot oven 15 minutes. Strain syrup from a quart can of apricots, mash ½ the fruit and sweeten to taste, spread between the layers and on top.

Strawberry Shortcake.

(Mrs. Rogers.)

Two teaspoonfuls baking powder sifted into 1 quart flour, scant ½ cup butter, 2 tablespoonfuls sugar, little salt, enough sweet milk or water to make a soft dough, roll out into two layers, placing one on the other with a little flour and butter between the layers. Bake 15 minutes. Separate the layers. Spread the bottom layer with strawberries previously sweetened with pulverized sugar. Whip the white of an egg to a froth, add 2 tablespoonfuls sugar, spread on top layer and dot with whole berries. Raspberry and peach shortcake can be made in same way.

Snow Drops.

One cup butter, 1 small cup milk, 2 cups sugar, 5 egg whites, 3 cups flour, 1 teaspoonful baking powder, 1 teaspoonful extract nutmeg or vanilla. Beat the butter and sugar to a cream, add the egg whites, well beaten, milk, baking powder and flour sifted together, and then the flavoring extract. Bake in small round tins.

Sand Tarts.

(Miss Wister.)

Three ounces Cottolene; 2 pounds flour; 2 pounds sugar; 3 eggs.

Cut the Cottolene up in the flour, then add the sugar and eggs; roll them; cut in squares; wet the top with a feather dipped in egg; put thin strips of the dough across the top, and sprinkle with powdered almonds and cinnamon.

Cocoanut Drops.

(Miss Wister.)

Two cups cocoanut; 1 cup sugar; 1 tablespoonful flour; 1 egg white, beaten stiff.

Drop on buttered paper and sift sugar over them; bake fifteen minutes in a slow oven.

Dominoes.

(Mrs. F. L. Gillette.)

Take 1 cup sugar; 1 egg; 1 cup sweet milk; 2 cups flour; 1 level tablespoonful cold Cottolene; 2 heaping teaspoonfuls baking powder; flavor to taste.

Have a plain cake baked in shallow biscuit tins, half an inch deep. When cool cut into small oblong pieces the size and shape of dominoes, a trifle larger. Frost the top and sides of each piece. When the frosting is hard enough, draw the lines and dots by dipping a camel's hair brush in chocolate icing, making them correspond with dominoes. Nice for children's parties, picnics, etc.

Lemon or Vanilla Cookies.

Two cups sugar, 1 cup Cottolene, ¾ cup sweet milk, 2 eggs, 5 cups of flour, 2 teaspoonfuls of baking power and a little salt, which must be sifted into the flour. Mix all together and add lemon or vanilla flavoring to taste. Sprinkle cocoanut on top. Roll very thin and bake quickly.

Doughnuts.

(Mrs. C. W. F.)

One quart of flour, 2 rounding teaspoonfuls baking power, 1 cup of milk, (sour milk may be used, with ½ teaspoonful soda), 1 cup sugar, 1 saltspoonful ground nutmeg or cinnamon, 1 saltspoonful salt, 2 eggs, 2 tablespoonfuls Cottolene (after it has been melted). Fry in hot Cottolene.

Hermits.

(Mrs. Wm. Merrill.)

One cup sugar, ½ cup milk, 1 cup butter, 3 eggs, 1 teaspoonful baking powder, 1 cup chopped raisins or currants, all kinds of spice, except ginger, flour to roll. If made of sour milk, use soda.

Sweedish Timbals.

(Mrs. L. M. C.)

One pint of flour less 2 tablespoonfuls, ½ pint sweet milk, 3 eggs, 2 tablespoonfuls olive oil, 1 teaspoonful salt, stir flour and milk to a perfectly smooth batter, add oil and salt, then eggs.

Lemon Queens.

(Mrs. Wm. Merrill.)

Four eggs, 1 cup sugar, ½ cup butter, 1¼ cups flour, ¼ teaspoonful soda, 1 tablespoonful lemon juice, and a little of the grated rind. Beat butter to a cream, add sugar gradually, then add grated rind and juice of the lemon, then yolks of eggs beaten, then the flour with the soda in it, then the beaten whites of the eggs. Bake in rings, and when taken from the oven, sprinkle with powdered sugar.

Ginger Snaps.

(Mrs. M. T. Allyn.)

One cup of molasses, 1 teaspoonful of soda, ⅔ of a cup of melted lard, teaspoonful of ginger, flour to make it stiff enough to roll out. Must be rolled very thin. Set the molasses on the stove, when it comes to a boil stir in the soda, then the ginger and lard, after which take from the stove and add the flour. Bake in hot oven.

Ginger Cookies.

(Clara Foggs.)

One cup of molasses put on the stove to boil, while this is boiling take ½ cup sugar, 1 egg, 1 teaspoonful of ginger, beat thoroughly 1 teaspoonful of soda, stir into the hot molasses dry, pour that slowly over the egg and stir quickly. Flour enough to roll smooth. Before you put flour in, put in 1 tablespoonful of vinegar.

Shrewsbury Cookies.

(Mrs. H. E. W.)

One pound flour, 1 pound sugar, ½ pound butter, 3 eggs, 2 teaspoonfuls ground cinnamon. Mix butter and flour, then add sugar and cinnamon. Mix into a paste with the eggs, roll out thin.

MEMORANDA.

D. E. Kleps & Co.

DEALERS IN

Fine Groceries, Meats and Provisions.

———o———

BUTTER, EGGS, AND DRIED FRUITS, CANNED GOODS AND PRESERVES.

———o———

CIGARS AND TOBACCO.

———o———

Telephone 1628.   Corner New Jersey Ave. and R St. N. W.

PRESERVES and JELLIES.

*"Give a husband what he likes,
And save a hundred household strikes."*
OLD RHYMES.

Strawberry Preserves.
(Miss Helen L. Johnson.)
[Editor *Table Talk*.]

Add 1 cup of boiling water to 2 pounds of granulated sugar, and stir over hot water until the sugar is dissolved. Put the kettle over the fire, add 2 pounds of strawberries, and simmer gently for 10 minutes, 5 minutes longer if the fruit does not look clear. Skim out the fruit very gently, lay on platters and put in the hot sun while the syrup is being boiled down. Boil the syrup until it is thick and rich, strain off any thin syrup caused by the standing of the berries in the sun, and add the berries to the thick syrup. Fill the cans and screw down the tops immediately.

Hodge Podge.
(Mrs. Keech.)

One half peck quinces, ½ peck pears, ½ peck peaches, ½ pound sugar and 1 gill water to each pound of fruit.

Tomato Figs.
(Miss Curry.)

Select quite ripe yellow pear tomatoes. Scald and remove the skins. Place the tomatoes in a porcelain kettle and cover with sugar, using ½ pound of sugar to each pound of fruit. Stew slowly over a moderate fire until the sugar has penetrated the fruit. Lifting each tomato carefully with a spoon, spread them on dishes and stand them in the sun 1 or 2 days to dry, sprinkling with granulated sugar several times during the drying. When perfectly dry pack in jars, with layers of sugar. Do not allow any moisture to fall on the fruit while drying.

Grape Jelly.

(Mrs. C. W. F.)

The grapes should be used before they get ripe, when they are just turning; stem and slightly cook them; then strain through a jelly bag, place the liquid again in the preserving kettle and allow it to come slowly to the boiling point; let it boil for 15 minutes, meanwhile skimming it with care; to every pint of juice now add 1 pound of granulated sugar which has been previously warmed in shallow pans but not allowed to melt; let the mixture boil 5 minutes and then pour into jelly glasses and set it away to cool.

Crabapple and currant jelly is made in the same way.

Cherry Jelly.

Dissolve a box of best gelatine in a pint of cold water for an hour, then add a pint of boiling cherry juice, and sugar to taste. Strain through a flannel jelly bag, and pour into the moulds that have been dipped in cold water. Place on ice and let them stand over night. When ready to serve, loosen the edges and turn on glass dishes.

Gooseberry Jam.

Time, 1¼ hours; ¾ pound loaf sugar to 1 pound red gooseberries. Pick off stalks and buds from gooseberries, bruise them lightly, boil them quickly for 3 to 10 minutes, stirring all the time; then add sugar, pounded and sifted to fruit, boil quickly, removing scum as it rises. Put into pots, when cold cover as above. All jams are made much in the same way.

Ice Cream Saloons,

721 6th St., Between G and H Streets, N. W.

WASHINGTON, D. C.

ICE CREAM AND WATER ICES.

PARTIES, RECEPTIONS, WEDDINGS, FAIRS, ETC.,
FURNISHED AT THE SHORTEST
NOTICE ON REASONABLE
TERMS.

E. J. BENTLEY,

DEALER IN

Coal, Coke and Wood,

FLOUR, HAY, GRAIN &c.

MAIN OFFICE AND YARD:

No. 1542 N. Capitol St., Cor. Florida Ave.

BRANCH OFFICE:

No. 1412 V St. N. W.

2240 POUNDS TO THE TON.

WOOD SAWED AND SPLIT

in any length and size, and kept under cover.

✸TERMS CASH.✹

CANDIES.

"Hold fast that which is good."

Granulated sugar is preferable. Candy should not be stirred while boiling. Cream tartar should not be added until syrup begins to boil. Butter should be put in when candy is almost done. Flavors are more delicate when not boiled in candy, but added afterward.

Never, when pouring out candy, scrape the saucepan over it, or allow any of the scrapings of the saucepan to fall into it. Always use a thick saucepan, in which to boil sugar.

French Candy.

(Mrs. Keech.)

Two and one-half pounds confectioner's sugar (4x), 1 pint grated cocoanut, white of 1 egg mixed in 1 tablespoonful cold water and a little flavoring. Knead like dough. Make out and mix with nuts.

Cream Candy.

(Mrs. J. F. Bancroft.)

One pound of sugar, 1 tablespoonful of vinegar, 1 cup of water. Flavor with vanilla; stir very little. When the candy stiffens by dropping a few drops in cold water, it is done. Pull until it grows white.

Candied Pop-Corn.

(Mrs. C. W. F.)

Put into an iron kettle 1 tablespoonful butter, 3 tablespoonfuls water, 1 teacupful white pulverized sugar. Boil until ready to candy, then throw in 3 quarts of nicely popped corn. Stir briskly till candy is evenly distributed over corn. Take kettle from fire, stir until it is cooled a little and you have each grain separate and crystallized with sugar, taking care that corn does not burn. Nuts of any kind prepared in same way.

Efferton Taffy.

(Mrs. A. G. Rogers.)

This is a favorite English confection. To make it, take 3 pounds of the best brown sugar and boil with 1½ pints of water, until the candy hardens in cold water. Then add ½ pound of sweet flavored fresh butter, which will soften the candy. Boil a few minutes until it again hardens and pour it into trays. Flavor with lemon if desired.

Peppermint.

(Mrs. James Campbell.)

Two cups granulated sugar, ½ cup of cold water. Let it boil three minutes. Beat in 6 tablespoonfuls of pulverized sugar, scant ½ teaspoonful of cream of tartar, 10 drops peppermint. Drop it with a teaspoon.

Caramels.

(E. J. F.)

Three pounds brown sugar, 1 cake chocolate, 1 cup milk, 1 cup water and good size piece butter. Flavor with vanilla. When done, beat 15 minutes; put in a pan; cut into squares when cool.

MISCELLANEOUS.

"Last but not least."

To Prepare Curry Powder.

One ounce ginger, 1 ounce mustard, 1 ounce pepper, 3 of coriander seed, 3 of turmeric, ¼ ounce cardamons, ¼ ounce cayenne pepper, ¼ ounce cinnamon, and ¼ ounce cumin seed. Pound fine, sift and cork tight in bottle.

Washing Fluid.

One pound Babbit's potash, 1 ounce salts of tartar, 1 ounce borax, 1 ounce ammonia, 4 quarts boiling water. Make in a tin or wooden bucket and bottle when cool. Use 1 teacupful to 3 pails of water, and a very little soap.

To Wash Blankets.

(Mrs. Gwathmey.)

Seven gallons water in boiler, ½ pound ivory soap dissolved in water. Add 2 tablespoonfuls kerosene oil. Let steam but not boil; rinse in two waters having the water warm; wring dry, shake well, hang in hot sun. This recipe will wash two large blankets. Keep in boiler about ½ hour, constantly stirring with a stick. No rubbing is necessary. Two grains of pulverized burnt alum added to 1 gallon of water, will cause turbid water to be as clear as well water.

PHONE 176 FOR
BREAD! BREAD! BREAD!

If you want good, clean, wholesome, palatable bread, use **B**OSTON **B**AKERY **B**READ. Wwe make all kinds, and use only the best, pure ingredients. Every loaf we make bears our label, accept none without it. Our latest production excells all other bread, we refer to our "Nickel Bread," nickel by name, and costs a nickel and is labeled "Boston Bakery Nickel Bread." Be sure to look for our name, as it will, like all good things, have many inferior imitations.

H. B. LEARY, Proprietor,

119, 121, 123 First Street. Foot of Capitol Grounds.

Notify us if your grocer doesn't sell our goods.

SCHOOL OF COOKERY,
1228 N STREET, N. W.

Lessons in all kinds of cookery are given to ladies and servants at moderate prices by MISS ADELAIDE PAYNE.

Mission Employment Bureau,
1228 N STREET, N. W.

Reliable servants both white and colored are furnished by MRS. E. J. DUVALL.
Fee, one dollar for ladies. Fifty cents for servants.

To Clarify Grease.

To clarify grease of any kind, cut a potato in slices, drop into the hot grease, fry a dark brown and your fat is pure and clean for cooking.

Brown Bread.

(Miss Adelaide Payne.)

(School Cookery.)

One cup of yellow Indian meal; 1 cup of Graham flour; 1 cup of sour milk; 2 cups of sweet milk; ½ a cup of molasses; 1 teaspoonful of soda; 1 scant teaspoonful of salt. Sift the Graham, then mix it with the Indian and rye. Stir the soda in the sour milk until thoroughly dissolved; add the salt, sweet milk, molasses and stir all into the dry mixture, beating until perfectly smooth. Grease your brown bread mold or tin, cover tightly and steam for five hours. If a hard crust is desired, steam four hours, then put in the oven for one hour.

Lemon Cream.

(Miss Adelaide Payne.)

(School Cookery.)

Four eggs; 6 tablespoonfuls of sugar; the grated rind of 1 lemon and 4 tablespoonfuls of lemon juice; 2 tablespoonfuls of hot water. Separate the yolks of the eggs from the whites. Beat the yolks light; then add 4 tablespoonfuls of granulated sugar, the lemon juice and rind. Stir well; then add the hot water, mixing all well together. Cook this mixture in a double boiler until it thickens, stirring all the time. Beat the whites of the eggs to a stiff froth and add 2 tablespoonfuls of *powdered* sugar, *cutting* it in. Remove the yolk mixture from the fire and cut in gently the whites, folding and cutting in, until the two are well mixed. Turn into a glass dish and serve very cold. If *too acid*, use less lemon juice.

Points About Salt.

Ink stains can be entirely removed by the immediate application of dry salt before the ink has dried. When the salt has become discolored by absorbing the ink, brush it off and apply more, wetting it slightly. Continue this until the ink is all removed.—Dampened salt will remove the discoloration of cups and saucers caused by tea and careless washing.—New calicoes and stockings should be allowed to lie in salt water for an hour before the the first wash, to set the colors.—To cool a hot dish quickly, set it in a pan full of cold salt water, which will cool it more rapidly than water free from salt.—A teaspoonful of salt in each kerosene lamp makes the oil give a clearer and much better light and it is claimed saves the oil as well.—Willow-ware can best be cleaned by a solution of salt and water.—To clean door matting, wash it with weak salt and water, and dry it well.—Salt dissolved in alcohol is often good for removing grease spots from cloth.—Salt will curdle new milk; so in preparing custard and porridges, salt should not be added until the last thing.—If your coal fire is low, throw on a tablespoonful of salt and it will help it very much.—To make whites of eggs beat quickly, put in a pinch of salt.

Hop Tea.

A large spoonful of hops, simmer in a pint of water. When strong enough, strain off and add white sugar. A quieting drink, excellent for nervous headache.

Polish for Old Furniture.

Alcohol ½ pint, shellac and rosin each ¼ ounce; after these have dissolved in the alcohol, add ½ pint linseed oil; shake well. Apply with a sponge or brush, or canton flannel, rubbing it well after the application, which gives a nice polish.

To Remove Tar.

Rub well with lard. Afterwards wash in warm water and soap.

INDEX TO ADVERTISERS.

Artist.—Mrs. C. W. Smiley, 943 Mass. ave.	21
Butter.—W. S. Detwilder, Center market.	33
E. T. Gibbons, K St. market.	37
Eiker, all markets.	25
D. WM. OYSTER, Center market.	50
G. W. Story, K St. market.	3
Bromo Pepsin.—All Druggists.	12
Baking Powder.—IMPERIAL, all grocers.	vi
Baths.—HOSFORD ELECTRIC, 918 H St., N. W.	82
Welcome Foot, Bentley's drug store.	94
Bakery.—Boston.	174
Bird Store.—E. S. Schmid, 712, 12th St., N. W.	17
Cyclopædia.—D. Appleton, 437 7th St., N. W.	108
Coal.—M. Sells, 1840 14th St., N. W.	170
V. BALDWIN JOHNSON, 1101 R. I. ave.	66
Johnson Bros., 1206 F St.	74
C. H. Burgess & Son, 8th and O Sts., N. W.	37
G. W. Merrill & Co., 454 N. Y. ave.	45
E. J. BENTLEY, 1412 V St., N. W.	170
Clothier.—Saks & Co., 7th and Market Space.	3
Confectioner and Ice Cream.—T. Jarvis, 426 9th St. N. W.	17
F. T. Budd, 510 9th St. N. W.	12
W. W. Wonn, 721 6th St.	169
F. Freund, 813 Tenth St.	79
Cottolene.—N. K. FAIRBANK Co.	IV
Cooking School.—1328 N St., N. W.	174
Dairy.—Eckington, 101 B St. S. E.	37
Brightwood, 10th and Mass. Ave.	7
Sampson's, 1003 N. Y. Ave.	12
Belmont, 1804 14th St.	70
Hartung's, Prospect St. N. E.	90
Dry Goods.—W. D. Clark & Co., 811 Market Space.	3-86

Dry Goods.—Carhart & Leidy, 928 7th St.	41
Druggists.—McComas, 1801 Vt. ave.	152
C. V. Dorman, 1007 H St., N. W.	7
Furniture.—H. Burkhart & Sons, 1017 7th St.	37
W. H. Hoeke, 801 Market Space.	90
Feed.—J. P. V. Ritter, 1321, 7th St., N. W.	25
Flour.—CERES, W. M. Galt & Co.	iv
Gas Stoves.—C. A. Mudiman, 614, 12th St., N. W.	152
Grocers. Provisions. Meats.—	
HART & HIGGINS, 11th and I Sts., N. W.	128
C. W. BARKER, 1210, F St.	136
KEECH & STRONG, 13th and W Sts., N. W.	112
C. S. Montague, 2204, 14th St.	118
H. S. Haight, 11th and S Sts., N. W.	94
J. H. Hungerford, 9th and O Sts., N. W.	45
C. M. Smoot, 3d and E Sts., N. E.	7
B. T. Trueworthy, Jr., K St. Market.	7
Bransom & Tarbell, 9th and H Sts., N. W.	12
Dorsey's Market, 10th and I Sts., N. W.	21
Lavender & Rott, Center Market.	25
L. A. Delwig, 2d and Mass. Av.	25-118
G. S. Perrie, N. Liberty Market.	33
Denham & White, 8th and S Sts., N. W.	54
EMRICH BEEF Co., Telephone 347.	28
Sam'l Fenton, N. Liberty Market.	21
J. F. Weyrick, O St. Market.	58
V. Ostmann, Center Market.	54
W. L Matthews, 10th & S Sts.	152
D. E. Kelps, Corner N. J. Ave. and R St. N. W.	166
Hatters and Furriers.—Stinemetz & Son, 1237 Pa. Ave.	118
Jeweler.—Chas. F. Plett, 1308 7th St. N. W.	33
Ice.—National Capital Ice Co.	108
Laundry.—YALE STEAM, Telephone 1092.	vii
Millinery.—Mrs. A. T. Whiting, 518 10th St. N. W.	62
Monumental, 939 F St. N. W.	62

Opticians.—Buchanan Bros. 1115 F St. N. W. — 41
Oysters.—R. M. Frost, 1500 8th St. N. W. — 58
Paints and Glass.—J. R. Riggles and Bro., 712 K St., N. W. — 3
    Chas. E. Hodgkin, 913 7th St. N. W. — 54
    R. M. Brown, 7th and N Sts. N. W. — 41
Paper Hanger.—Geo. S. Donn, 1240 7th St., N. W. — 45
    G. Y. Hansell, 601 H St. N. E. — 86
Patents.—W. W. Curry, Washington, D. C. — 70
Printing.—Age Printing Co., 8th and H Sts. — 94
Periodicals.—Microscopical Pub. Co., Washington, D. C. — 41
    Our Church Magazine. — III
Photographs.—J. D. BOYCE, 1113 F St., N. W. — ii
Real Estate and Fire Ins.—G. A. Jorden, 1417 F St. — 58
    WESCOTT & WILCOX, 1907 Pa. ave. — 100
Sewing Machines.—S. Oppenheimer, 514 9th St., N. W. — 62
    STANDARD SEWING MACHINE. — 146
Shoes.—Warren Shoe House, 919 F St. — 74
    STOLL'S SHOE PALACE, 810 F St. N. W. — iii
Summer Resort.—A Fisher, 138 E St., N. E. — 17
Tailors.—SNYDER & WOOD, 1111 Pa. ave. — 104
    J. J. Costinett, 624 14th St. — 90
Typewriter.—J. C. Parker (Hammond), 619 7th St. — 94
Undertaker.—J. Wm. Lee, 332 Pa ave. — 78
    J. R. Wright, 1337 10th St., N. W. — 68

www.ingramcontent.com/pod-product-compliance
Lightning Source LLC
Chambersburg PA
CBHW032148160426
43197CB00008B/820